"WHY" SOUP'S ON!?

AS I WORK WITH GOLFERS, COACHING THEM TO IMPROVE THEIR MENTAL GAMES, I WITNESS AN INTERESTING COMMON TREND. PLAYERS, FROM THE WEEKEND WARRIOR TO THE TOURING PROFESSIONAL, CONTINUOUSLY REPORT THAT THEY AREN'T GETTING ENOUGH QUALITY FROM THEIR PRACTICE TIME. IF I HAD A DOLLAR FOR EACH TIME I HAVE HEARD A PLAYER TELL ME, "I AM TERRIFIC IN PRACTICE, BUT HAVE TROUBLE TRANSLATING MY RANGE SUCCESS ONTO THE COURSE," I WOULD BE, WELL, NEARLY WEALTHY. IT'S A COMMON PROBLEM FOR GOLFERS. THE SOLUTION IS, I AM PLEASED TO SAY, AT YOUR FINGERTIPS.

MOST GOLFERS, YOU SEE, DO NOT SPEND ENOUGH TIME PRACTICING. AND, WHEN THEY DO, THEY AREN'T IN THE CORRECT FRAME OF MIND TO LEARN EFFECTIVELY. I BELIEVE THAT IF GOLF PRACTICE WERE MORE FUN, INSTEAD OF RAPID-FIRE-BALL-BEATING OR MUNDANE MECHANICAL REPETITION, PLAYERS WOULD FIND THEIR WAY TO THE LOCAL PRACTICE FACILITY MORE OFTEN. ALSO, PLAYERS SELDOM REACH A "THIS MATTERS" MINDSET DURING PRACTICE BECAUSE, WELL, IT DOESN'T. THE ONLY CONSEQUENCE TO A POOR SHOT IS ANOTHER ATTEMPT. IN OTHER WORDS, THE COMPETITIVENESS OF AN ACTUAL ROUND ISN'T SIMULATED IN PRACTICE.

OVER 50 OF CHICAGOLAND'S BEST PGA & LPGA TEACHERS HAVE OFFERED THEIR PERSONAL FAVORITE SHORT-GAME PRACTICE GAME IN ORDER TO HELP YOU HAVE MORE FUN WHILE PRACTICING AND TO HELP YOU REACH THE "THIS MATTERS" MINDSET DURING PRACTICE. IN ADDITION, I HAVE SPRINKLED SOME SPORT PSYCHOLOGY ANECDOTES AND "WORDS OF WISDOM" THROUGHOUT SOUPS ON! THE END RESULT, I AM CONFIDENT, WILL BE MORE ENJOYMENT AT THE RANGE AND GREATER SUCCESS ON THE COURSE.

SOUPS ON! CHICAGO.

Michael

MICHAEL RIGGS, M.ED.

Publication #9082

Printed in the United States of America by:

G & R Publishing Company
507 Industrial Street
Waverly, IA 50677
800-383-1679
gandr@gandrpublishing.com
http://www.cookbookprinting.com

List of Chefs

DR. JIM SUTTIE, PGA
GARY GROH, PGA
DAN KOCHEVAR, PGA
JOHN ESPOSITO, PGA
MARGIE MUZIK, LPGA
BETTY KAUFMAN, LPGA
JOHN SWAN, PGA
TOM O'CONNOR, PGA
DAVE ERICKSON, PGA
MIKE HOLUB, PGA
CASEY BROZEK, PGA
HARLAN CHEMERS, PGA
PENNI GODDEN, LPGA
RENIE CALKIN, LPGA
RICH LORENZ, PGA
RACHEL TERESI, LPGA
BRYAN LUEDKE, PGA
JOHN PARSONS, PGA
CAROL RHOADES, LPGA
DENNIS JOHNSEN, PGA
MICHAEL JONES, PGA
PETE LATKIEWICZ, PGA
JASON ASLANIAN, PGA
DOUG BAUMAN, PGA
JOHN CLELAND, PGA
JIM KARRAS, PGA
JIM VOGT, PGA

MICHAEL HARRIGAN, PGA
MICHAEL SMALL, PGA
PRESTON IRWIN, PGA
JOHN CRAIG, PGA
CONNIE DEMATTIA, PGA
BILL ABRAMS, PGA
BILL BROLLEY, PGA
CRAIG CARNEY, PGA
MARK ESLER, PGA
KELLY HOLMES, PGA
DANNY MULHEARN, PGA
DAVID IMPASTATO, PGA
MARALEE MALANEY, LPGA
NOEL ALLEN, PGA
RICK JOHNSON, PGA
TIM O'NEAL, PGA
TOM EVERS, PGA
MATT ABRAMAVICIUS, PGA
SCOTT SANDFORT, PGA
BRIAN MORRISON, PGA
MARK LABIAK, PGA
TIM SURLAS, PGA
BILLY KLEMZ, PGA
DAVE O'NEAL, PGA
BRUCE PATTERSON, PGA
CHRIS HEASLEY, PGA
BILLY NESTEL, PGA

THANKS, CHEFS !!!

Putting

BASEBALL

"BASEBALL" IS BEST PLAYED WITH A PARTNER. BUT, YOU COULD PLAY BY YOURSELF TRYING TO BEAT YOUR PERSONAL BEST RUNS SCORED. EITHER WAY, IT'S A LOT OF FUN !

EACH PLAYER POSITONS HIMSELF NEAR A CUP. THE FARTHER THE CUPS ARE APART, THE FEWER THE NUMBER OF RUNS THAT WILL BE SCORED.

PLAYER ONE IS UP TO BAT FIRST. HE PUTTS TO PLAYER TWO'S CUP. SCORING GOES LIKE THIS:

SINGLE... IF THE PUTT STOPS WITHIN ONE PUTTER HEAD OF THE HOLE,

DOUBLE... IF THE PUTT STOPS OUTSIDE ONE PUTTER HEAD OF THE HOLE, BUT LIPPED OUT (TOUCHED THE RIM OF THE HOLE).

TRIPLE... IF THE PUTT STOPS WITHIN ONE PUTTER HEAD OF THE HOLD AFTER LIPPING OUT.

HOME RUN... IF THE PUTT IS HOLED.

OUT... ANY OTHER PUTT.

THREE OUTS MEAN THAT HALF AN INNING IS OVER AND PLAYER TWO PUTTS AT PLAYER ONE'S CUP. BASE RUNNERS ADVANCE AS THEY WOULD IN REGULAR BASEBALL. PLAYERS SWITCH CUPS BETWEEN INNINGS.

DECIDE BEFORE YOU START HOW MANY INNINGS WILL BE PLAYED. "BASEBALL" WILL STRENGTHEN YOUR PUTTING SKILLS UNDER PRESSURE.

PLAY BALL !!!

MARK ESLER, PGA
ROYAL MELBOURNE COUNTRY CLUB
847.913.8380

Notes

 # CROQUET

THIS GAME IS PLAYED MUCH LIKE THE LAWN GAME CRO-QUET, WITH A FEW TWISTS.

CROQUET IS BEST PLAYED WITH A PARTNER OR TWO. ROUND UP A COUPLE OF OTHER PEOPLE THAT ARE ALSO PRACTICING AND CHALLENGE THEM TO A FRIENDLY LITTLE GAME!

THE OBJECTIVE IS TO SINK PUTTS, MOVING FROM CUP TO CUP ON THE PRACTICE GREEN, ALONG AN AGREED UPON PATH. THE FIRST PLAYER TO COMPLETE THE COURSE WINS!

EVERYONE STARTS FROM THE SAME SPOT ON THE PRAC-TICE GREEN. PLAYER ONE PUTTS TO THE FIRST HOLE. IF PLAYER ONE MAKES HIS PUTT, HE GETS A FREE STROKE TO THE NEXT HOLE. SIMPLY REMOVE THE BALL FROM THE CUP AND SET THE BALL ONE PUTTER-HEAD LENGTH FROM THE CUP, NO CLOSER TO THE NEXT HOLE. IF PLAYER ONE MISSES HIS PUTT IT IS THEN PLAYER TWO'S TURN, THEN PLAYER THREE, ETC. A PLAYER MAY "BUMP" ANOTHER PLAYER'S BALL AND RECEIVE A FREE STROKE AT ANY TIME. "BUMPED" BALLS ARE TO BE PLAYED AS THEY LIE.

CONTINUE PUTTING, IN TURN, UNTIL ONE PLAYER FINISHES THE COURSE.

THERE IS A DEFINITE STRATEGY TO "CROQUET." USE YOUR "BUMPS" WISELY AND NEVER UNDER-ESTIMATE THE CRUEL NATURE OF YOUR FRIENDLY OPPONENT. ALL IS FAIR IN LOVE AND CROQUET!

MICHAEL HARRIGAN, PGA
MEDINAH COUNTRY CLUB
630.438.6801

Notes

CONNECT THE DOTS

THIS MAY BE THE SIMPLEST, YET MOST EFFECTIVE PUTTING GAME YOU WILL EVER PLAY.

THE OBJECTIVE OF "CONNECT THE DOTS" IS TO WORK YOUR WAY AROUND THE PRACTICE PUTTING GREEN, FROM HOLE TO HOLE, MERRILY TWO-PUTTING AS YOU GO. A THREE-PUTT SENDS YOU BACK TO THE BEGINNING.

YOU WILL ONLY NEED ONE BALL AND YOUR PUTTER FOR THIS GAME. START ANYWHERE YOU WISH ON THE GREEN AND PUTT TO ANY HOLE. IF YOU ONE-PUTT, YOU HAVE EARNED YOURSELF A "CREDIT" STROKE TO BE USED TO ERASE A THREE-PUTT. IF YOU NEED 2 PUTTS, YOU MAY CONTINUE. IF YOU NEED 3 PUTTS YOU MAY USE A "CREDIT" AND CONTINUE. IF YOU MISS YOUR SECOND PUTT AND YOU DON'T HAVE A CREDIT, YOU MUST GO BACK TO THE BEGINNING.

CONTINUE "CONNECTING THE DOTS" UNTIL YOU HAVE PUTTED INTO ALL OF THE CUPS.

TO SPICE THE GAME UP A BIT, YOU CAN PUTT TO THE FARTHEST POSSIBLE HOLE OR NEVER PUTT TO AN ADJACENT HOLE. WHILE "CONNECT THE DOTS" IS SIMPLE, IT IS VERY EFFECTIVE FOR IMPROVING YOUR PUTTING. BE SURE TO USE YOUR FULL PUTTING ROUTINE AS YOU PRACTICE. THE BETTER YOU PRACTICE THE BETTER YOU WILL PLAY.

BRUCE PATTERSON
BUTLER NATIONAL COUNTRY CLUB

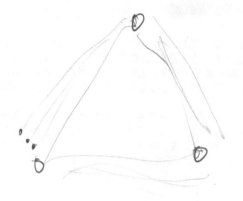

3 putts   -1 pt.
2 putts   +1 pt.
1 putt   +2 pts.

 # NO MORE THREE-PUTTS

FOR "NO MORE THREE-PUTTS" YOU WANT TO PICK OUT THREE OR FOUR HOLES ON THE PRACTICE GREEN THAT FORM A TRIANGLE OR A SQUARE. IT IS BEST IF THE HOLES ARE ABOUT 20-30 FEET APART.

USING THREE BALLS, START AT ONE OF THE HOLES AND PUTT IN A CLOCKWISE DIRECTION AROUND THE HOLES THAT YOU HAVE CHOSEN. PUTT-OUT EACH OF THE THREE BALLS TRYING NOT TO THREE PUTT. IF YOU AVOID A THREE-PUTT, GIVE YOURSELF THREE POINTS. IF YOU THREE-PUTT ANY OF THE THREE BALLS YOU RECEIVE NO POINTS FOR THE HOLE. PUTT TO THE NEXT HOLE AND REPEAT THE SCORING SYSTEM. THEN PUTT AGAIN, THE THIRD AND FOURTH HOLES.

HOW DID YOU DO?

> 12 POINTS... MASTER PUTTER
> 9 POINTS... PRETTY DARN GOOD
> 6 POINTS... IT'S PRACTICE TIME
> 3 POINTS... IT'S <u>REALLY</u> PRACTICE TIME

"NO MORE THREE-PUTTS" WILL HELP YOU TO DEVELOP DISTANCE CONTROL AND WILL IMPROVE YOUR ABILITY TO PUTT UNDER PRESSURE... ESPECIALLY ON THE SHORT ONES THAT MEAN 3 POINTS!

PUTT TO WIN !!!

MIKE HOLUB, PGA
THE GLEN CLUB
847.724.7272

Notes

 # DUNK IT

"DUNK IT" IS A GREAT GAME TO HELP YOU MASTER THOSE 6 FOOT PUTTS THAT WILL TURN AN AVERAGE ROUND INTO A GOOD ONE, AND A GOOD ROUND INTO A GREAT ONE. CONSISTENTLY MAKING SIX-FOOTERS WILL MAKE YOUR DAY.

DROP THREE BALLS SIX FEET FROM A HOLE OF YOUR CHOICE ON THE PRACTICE GREEN. THREE PUTTS EQUALS ONE HOLE OF GOLF. WITH FULL PUTTING ROUTINE, ATTEMPT TO MAKE EACH OF THE THREE PUTTS.

SCORING GOES AS FOLLOWS:

> ZERO PUTTS MADE... DOUBLE BOGIE
> 1 PUTT MADE... BOGIE
> 2 PUTTS MADE... PAR
> 3 PUTTS MADE... BIRDIE

PLAY EITHER 18 OR 36 HOLES. IF YOU ARE PLAYING BIRDIE GOLF YOU ARE VERY GOOD. IF NOT, GET "DUNKING" TO IMPROVE THE MOST IMPORTANT CLUB IN YOUR BAG... YOUR PUTTER.

"DUNK IT" WILL HELP YOU TO CONCENTRATE ON EVERY PUTT BECAUSE EVERY PUTT COUNTS... JUST LIKE IN COMPETITION. ON THE COURSE YOU ARE ALWAYS TRYING TO SAVE BOGEY, PAR, OR MAKE A BIRDIE, RIGHT? WELL, IT IS BEST TO TRAIN YOURSELF FOR COMPETITION IN PRACTICE.

KELLY HOLMES, PGA
BITTERSWEET GOLF CLUB
847.855.9031

Notes

FIRST IN

"FIRST IN" IS A TWO-PLAYER PUTTING GAME THAT WILL TEST YOUR ABILITY TO RELAX AND STAY FOCUSED.

TWO HOLES ARE NEEDED, APPROXIMATELY 15 FEET APART. STANDING NEXT TO A HOLE, EACH PLAYER HAS THREE BALLS WITH WHICH HE PUTTS AS QUICKLY, OR SLOWLY, AS HE SEES FIT. THE OBJECTIVE IS TO BE THE FIRST TO MAKE A PUTT IN THE OPPOSITE HOLE. ONCE A PLAYER MAKES A PUTT, THE PLAYERS QUICKLY CHANGE POSITIONS AND CONTINUE PUTTING.

THE FIRST PLAYER TO SEVEN WINS !!!

YOU COULD INCREASE THE DIFFICULTY OF "FIRST IN" BY SELECTING TWO HOLES THAT ARE FARTHER APART OR ARE ON SEVERE SLOPES.

VERY OFTEN PLAYERS FEEL "RUSHED" WHILE THEY ARE PUTTING OR ARE PREPARING TO PUTT. THIS FEELING OFTEN TRANSLATES INTO A HURRIED OR RUSHED PUTTING STROKE. "FIRST IN" WILL HELP YOU TO STAY FOCUSED AND RELAXED DESPITE THE FACT THAT THE QUICKER YOU PUTT THE MORE OPPORTUNITIES YOU WILL HAVE TO WIN. REMEMBER, IT'S ABOUT QUALITY, NOT QUANTITY, ESPECIALLY WHEN YOU ARE PUTTING.

HARLAN CHEMERS, PGA
CONWAY FARMS GOLF CLUB
847.234.7160

Notes

On Challenge

CHALLENGE ISN'T DECIDING TO CLEAR THE WATER
WITH A FAIRWAY THREE-IRON
TO A DIME SIZED GREEN.
CHALLENGE ISN'T BEING DETERMINED TO STRIPE
A DRIVE THROUGH A NARROW CHUTE OF PINES.
CHALLENGE ISN'T VISUALIZING A SWEEPING FLOP SHOT
OVER A GREENSIDE BUNKER
TO A TIGHT FLAGSTICK.
TRUE CHALLENGE LIES IN STAYING FOCUSED ON
THE PROCESS OF CLEARING, STRIPING, AND SWEEPING
WHILE KNOWING THE PERIL THAT LOOMS
OFF OF THE GREEN, IN THE PINES, AND IN THE BUNKER.
THAT'S THE TRUE CHALLENGE.

Notes

FRINGE BENEFITS

"FRINGE BENFEITS" IS A GREAT GAME TO IMPROVE YOUR OVERALL FEEL ON THE GREEN AND TO IMPROVE YOUR MID-RANGE PUTTING DISTANCE CONTROL AND CONFIDENCE.

ON THE PRACTICE PUTTING GREEN, PLACE A TEE IN THE GROUND ABOUT TEN FEET FROM THE FRINGE. STANDING AT THE TEE, PACE OFF 10 STEPS, MOVING IN A LINE AWAY FROM THE FRINGE AND THE TEE. DROP SIX BALLS ON THE GREEN. YOU ARE NOW READY FOR SOME "FRINGE BENEFITS".

THE OBJECTIVE IS TO PUTT TOWARD THE FRINGE WITH EACH SUCCESSIVE PUTT LANDING AS CLOSE TO, BUT PAST, THE PREVIOUS PUTT, WITHOUT TOUCHING THE FRINGE. YOU MUST FIRST PUTT A BALL PAST THE TEE IN ORDER TO OPEN THE GAME. EACH SUCCESSIVE PUTT THAT PASSES THE PREVIOUS PUTT- AFTER YOUR OPENER - IS WORTH ONE, THEN TWO, THEN THREE, ETC. POINTS UNTIL YOU ARE OUT OF BALLS OR HIT THE FRINGE. ADD UP YOUR TOTAL SCORE.

13-15 POINTS... AWESOME!
10-12 POINTS... GOOD CONTROL.
8-9 POINTS... GETTING THE FEEL.
5-7 POINTS... ROOM

GREAT LAG PUTTING IS ONE OF THE SIGNS OF A GREAT PLAYER. EXCELLENT LAG & MIDDLE-DISTANCE CONTROL (20-30 FEET) WILL TRANSLATE INTO MORE SHORT PAR ATTEMPTS. OFTEN, A THREE-PUTT GREEN IS THE RESULT OF A POOR LAG THAT DOESN'T GIVE YOU A GOOD CHANCE TO DROP YOUR PAR PUTT.

DAVID IMPASTATO, PGA
ST. CHARLES COUNTRY CLUB
630.377.9340

Notes

 **GRADUATION**

 PLACE A COIN ONE PUTTERLENGTH FROM THE HOLE. YOU MUST MAKE 10 PUTTS IN A ROW TO GRADUATE. IF YOU MISS A PUTT AT ANY POINT, YOU MUST START OVER! AFTER COMPLETION, MOVE YOUR COIN AN ADDITIONAL PUTTERLENGTH AWAY FROM THE HOLE AND MAKE 8 IN A ROW. ONCE AGAIN, IF YOU MISS AT ANY POINT YOU MUST START OVER FROM THAT DISTANCE. MOVE YOUR COIN ANOTHER PUTTERLENGTH AND MAKE 4 IN A ROW. MOVE ONE MORE PUTTERLENGTH AND MAKE 2 IN A ROW. AND FINALLY, MOVE ONE MORE PUTTERLENGTH (WOW, 18 FEET) AND MAKE ONE PUTT TO GRADUATE !!!

HOW LONG SHOULD IT TAKE YOU TO GRADUATE?

>LESS THAN 45 MINUTES... PRO
>45-60 MINUTES... CLUB CHAMP
>60-90 MINUTES... SINGLE DIGIT HANDICAP
>MORE THAN 90 MINUTES... KEEP TRYING !!!

 KEEP YOUR EYES AND HEAD STILL WITH BOTH HANDS UNTIL THE BALL STOPS (HOPEFULLY IN THE HOLE). DO NOT PEEK TOO SOON. LISTEN FOR THE BALL TO FALL INTO THE HOLE. YOU ARE MOVING YOU R EYES IF YOU SEE A SHORT ONE GO IN.

"GRADUATION" WILL HELP YOU TO BE PATIENT, GAIN CONFIDENCE, CONCENTRATE, AND CONTROL YOUR TEMPER!

 DAVE ERICKSON, PGA
ST. ANDREWS GOLF CLUB
630.231.3100

Notes

HORSESHOES

"HORSESHOES" IS A GREAT GAME TO PLAY TO DEVELOP YOUR LAG PUTTING SKILLS.

WHILE YOU COULD CERTAINLY PLAY "HORSESHOES" BY YOURSELF, IT IS MOST FUN AND CHALLENGING WITH A PLAYING PARTNER. ALL PUTTS SHOULD BE LONGER THAN 30 FEET TO GET THE MOST BENEFIT FROM THIS GAME.

EACH PLAYER PLAYS WITH TWO BALLS. PLAYER "A" STARTS BY PUTTING TO A MUTUALLY DECIDED HOLE ON THE PUTTING GREEN. NEXT, PLAYER "B" PUTTS, TRYING TO GET HIS PUTT CLOSER TO THE HOLE THAN PLAYER "A." REPEAT WITH THE SECOND BALL. REMEMBER, KNOCK-OUTS (BUMPING YOUR OPPONENT AWAY FROM THE CUP) ARE COMPLETELY LEGAL IN "HORSESHOES". ONLY THE PLAYER CLOSEST TO THE HOLE (OR IN) CAN GAIN POINTS IN A ROUND.

POINTS ARE ACCUMULATED, AND LOST, AS SUCH:

> HOLED PUTT (RINGER) ... 3 POINTS
> WITHIN 1 FEET OF CUP... 2 POINTS
> WITHIN 2 FEET OF CUP... 1 POINT
> THE FARTHEST AWAY... -1 POINT

THE FIRST PLAYER TO 15 POINTS WINS !!!

EXCELLENT LAG PUTTING IS VERY IMPORTANT... ESPECIALLY WHEN IT COMES TO SAVING PARS. "HORSESHOES" WILL GIVE YOU BETTER FEEL FOR YOUR DISTANCE CONTROL WITH YOUR LAGS AND WILL IMPROVE YOUR CONFIDENCE IN YOUR ABILITY TO "GET IT CLOSE."

CASEY BROZEK, PGA
CRYSTAL LAKE COUNTRY CLUB
815.459.1068

Notes

JUST SHORT

"JUST SHORT" IS A GREAT GAME TO IMPROVE YOUR SPEED CONTROL AND FEEL FOR PUTTING.

THE OBJECT OF THE GAME IS TO PUTT EACH BALL A LITTLE SHORTER THAN THE PREVIOUS PUTT AND ACCUMULATE POINTS AS YOU GO.

ARRANGE 15 BALLS ON THE PRACTICE GREEN IN A SMALL PILE. PLACE A TARGET (HEAD COVER, TEE, ETC.) ABOUT 30 FEET AWAY FROM THE PILE. NOW, IT'S TIME TO COME UP "JUST SHORT."

PUTT THE FIRST BALL TOWARD THE TARGET, INTENDING TO HAVE IT STOP JUST SHORT. IF YOUR FIRST PUTT COMES UP SHORT, REGARDLESS OF HOW SHORT, GIVE YOURSELF A POINT. IF IT GOES PAST THE TARGET, SUBTRACT A POINT. NOW, REPEAT THIS PROCESS USING THE PREVIOUS BALL AS THE NEW TARGET. THE GAME IS OVER WHEN YOU HAVE PUTTED ALL 15 BALLS.

SCORING

13-15 POINTS... PROFESSIONAL SPEED CONTROL
11-12 POINTS... EXCELLENT SPEED CONTROL
8-10 POINTS... YOU'RE GETTING THE HANG OF IT!
LESS THAN 8... KEEP PRACTICING, YOU'LL GET IT.

MAKE PRACTICE COUNT !!!

TO MAKE "JUST SHORT" MORE DIFFICULT, PLACE THE TARGET A SHORTER DISTANCE AWAY OR USE MORE BALLS. DON'T BE SO CONCERNED WITH LINE, INSTEAD FOCUS ON THE FEEL OF THE SPEED AND LEARN TO PRODUCE VERY SUBTLE SPEED CHANGES.

RICK JOHNSON, PGA
NIKE GOLF LEARNING CENTER
708.449.6767

Notes

OPEN & SHUT CASE

"OPEN & SHUT CASE" WILL IMPROVE YOUR ABILITY TO MAKE SHORT (3 FOOT) PUTTS AND WILL BOOST YOUR ABILITY TO TRUST YOUR STROKE WHEN THE MATCH IS ON THE LINE.

PLACE ONE BALL AT THREE FEET FROM THE HOLE AT FOUR DIFFERENT POSITIONS: 12, 3, 6, AND 9 O'CLOCK, FOR A TOTAL OF FOUR BALLS. IT SHOULD LOOK LIKE THIS:

STARTING AT 12 O'CLOCK AND ADVANCING TO EACH SUCCESSIVE POSITION, WITH FULL ROUTINE, ATTEMPT TO PUTT THE BALL INTO THE HOLE. NEXT, REPLACE THE FOUR BALLS TO THEIR STARTING POSITIONS, EXECUTE YOUR FULL ROUTINE, BUT BEFORE YOU TAKE THE CLUB HEAD BACK, CLOSE YOUR EYES AND DON'T OPEN THEM UNTIL YOU HEAR THE BALL DROP INTO THE CUP.

GIVE YOURSELF 1 POINT FOR EACH OPEN-EYED, AND 2 POINTS FOR EACH CLOSED-EYED MADE PUTT. A SCORE OF 10 OR BETTER IS VERY GOOD !!!

PUTTING WITH YOUR EYES CLOSED IS A GREAT WAY TO IMPROVE YOUR ABILITY TO TRUST YOUR STROKE, AND STAY "PRESENT" AND CALM.

RICH LORENZ, PGA
INVERNESS GOLF CLUB
847.359.0244

Notes

24

 **Recipe**

SEVENS

 **Ingredients**

"SEVENS" IS A GREAT TWO-PLAYER PUTTING GAME THAT WILL IMPROVE YOUR ABILITY TO LAG PUTT VERY CLOSE TO THE HOLE... AND MAKE A FEW LONG ONES, TOO!

THE OBJECT OF "SEVENS" IS TO GAIN SEVEN POINTS, ON THE NOSE, BY OUT-PUTTING YOUR COMPETITION. EACH PLAYER WILL NEED ONE BALL AND THEIR PUTTER.

THE TALLER PLAYER CHOOSES THE TARGET HOLE AND HAS THE OPTION TO PUTT FIRST OR SECOND. EACH PLAYER WILL PUTT TO THE HOLE WITH SCORING DECIDED AS FOLLOWS:

    1 PT...   CLOSEST TO THE HOLE
    2 PTS...   SINK THE PUTT (IF BOTH PLAYERS
               SINK THE PUTT, THE SECOND PLAYER
               WINS)
    -1 PT....   THREE PUTT

THE PLAYER THAT IS TRAILING THE TOTAL SCORE GETS TO CALL THE NEXT PUTT AND CHOOSES TO PUTT FIRST OR SECOND. IF THE SCORE IS TIED, THE LOSER OF THE PREVIOUS HOLE GETS TO CALL HOLE AND ORDER.

 **Tips**

SOME PLAYERS LIKE TO PUTT SECOND, SO THAT THEY CAN SEE THE LINE FROM THE FIRST PLAYER'S PUTT. OTHERS CHOOSE TO PUT THE PRESSURE ON BY PUTTING FIRST. THIS IS A MATTER OF CHOICE. EITHER WAY, BE AGGRESSIVE AND FORCE YOUR OPPONENT INTO A MISTAKE.

 **Chef**

MARK LABIAK
RUTH LAKE COUNTRY CLUB

Notes

On Dreams

AT THE DAWN OF EACH NEW GOLF SEASON MOST
PLAYERS, FROM THE LOW TO THE HIGH HANDICAPPER,
WHISPER TO THEMSELVES, "THIS IS THE YEAR I GET IT ALL
STRAIGHTENED OUT. NO MORE TALK OF 'POTENTIAL.'
THIS IS THE YEAR OF STRAIGHT DRIVES,
SOFT IRONS, AND A STEELY PUTTER."
AND YET, "NEXT SEASON" BECOMES THE ANNUAL AUTUMN
MANTRA FOR THE PLAYER AS HE PLACES HIS CLUBS INTO
FORCED HYBERNATION IN THE CORNER OF THE GARAGE.
MAKING THOSE DREAMS OF HAVING A GREAT GOLF
GAME BECOME A REALITY IS THE PRODUCT OF A
CREATIVE AND INTELLIGENT PLAN EXECUTED WITH
COMMITMENT OVER THE LONG-HAUL, ALL
ENVELOPED WITHIN A GREAT ATTITUDE.
GOT GAME?

Notes

Ingredients

"13" IS A TWO-PLAYER PUTTING GAME THAT REQUIRES STRATEGY, GOOD DISTANCE CONTROL ,AND THE ABILITY TO SINK THE PRESSURE PUTT.

THERE ARE THREE WAYS TO SCORE:

1) CLOSEST TO THE HOLE (1 POINT)
2) MAKE THE PUTT (2 POINTS)
3) MAKE A PUTT ON TOP OF YOUR OPPONENT'S BALL (4 POINTS)
   NOTE: ONLY THE LAST BALL IN THE HOLE GETS THE 4 POINTS

EACH PLAYER WILL PUTT TWO BALLS TO A DESIGNATED HOLE.. PLAYER ONE PUTTS FIRST AND LAST. PLAYER TWO PUTTS SECOND AND THIRD. THE LOSER OF THE PREVIOUS HOLE CHOOSES THE NEXT CUP AND DECIDES IF HE WANTS TO PUTT FIRST OR SECOND. IF BALLS MAKE CONTACT WITH EACH OTHER, THEY WILL BE PLAYED AS THEY LIE. THE WINNER MUST HIT 13 EXACTLY. IF A PLAYER GOES OVER 13, HE MUST START OVER AT ZERO.

Tips

VERY OFTEN, WHEN PUTTING, PLAYERS DO NOT KEEP THEIR HEAD STILL . THIS IS USUALLY Y DUE TO THE FACT THAT THEY ARE TOO ANXIOUS TO SEE WHERE THE BALL IS GOING TO END UP. TRUST ME, IT IS GOING SOMEWHERE; TAKING AN EARLY LOOK WILL ONLY HURT ITS CHANCES OF PROPER ARRIVAL.

Chef

PETE LATKIEWICZ
AURORA COUNTRY CLUB
630.892.3785

Notes

THAT'S ODD

"THAT'S ODD" WILL HELP SHOW YOU THAT BEING MECHANICALLY MINDED WHILE PUTTING ISN'T THE BEST WAY TO MAKE GREAT PUTTS.
IT'S ABOUT THE TARGET !!!

BRING A SMALL BUCKET OF BALLS TO THE PRACTICE GREEN. CHOOSE A HOLE WITHOUT A LOT OF SLOPE. START BY PUTTING FROM THREE FEET OR ONE PUTTER LENGTH FROM THE HOLE. FOR THE ODD NUMBERED PUTTS (1.3.5, ETC.) LOOK AT THE BALL WHEN PUTTING. FOR THE EVEN NUMBERED PUTTS (2,4,6, ETC.) LOOK AT THE HOLE WHEN YOU STROKE THE PUTT. PUTT 20 BALLS TOTAL.

DID YOU MAKE MORE PUTTS WITH YOUR EYES ON THE BALL? OR, ON THE TARGET?

"THAT'S ODD" HELPS TO ILLUSTRATE THAT BEING AWARE OF THE TARGET, NOT THE BALL OR THE ME-CHANICS OF STROKING THE BALL, WILL HELP YOUR PUTTING TREMENDOUSLY.

Tips

WHEN YOU PLAY DARTS, DO YOU LOOK AT THE TIP OF THE DART AS YOU PREPARE TO THROW? OR, DO YOU THINK ABOUT YOUR ELBOW POSITION OR THE FINGERTIP PRESSURE ON THE DART BODY? OF COURSE NOT. WHY THEN DO PLAYERS GET HUNG UP ON THE PUTTER HEAD MOVING BACK AND FORTH STRAIGHT OR THE MECHANICS OF THEIR STROKE?

Chef

BRIAN MORRISON
OLYMPIA FIELDS COUNTRY CLUB
708.283.7663

Notes

PUSH N' TIME

"PUSH N' TIME" IS DESIGNED TO HELP YOU TO FEEL THE ACCELERATION OF THE PUTTER HEAD THROUGH IMPACT.

PLACE TWELVE BALLS IN A CIRCLE, EACH ABOUT THREE FEET AWAY, AROUND A SLOPING PUTTING HOLE. IMAGINE THAT THE PLACEMENT OF THE BALLS IS LIKE THE NUMBERS ON A FACE OF A CLOCK. THE BALL PLACED AT 12 O'CLOCK SHOULD BE AT THE TOP OF THE SLOPE, OR ABOVE THE HOLE. THE 6 O'CLOCK BALL SHOULD BE DIRECTLY BELOW THE HOLE. THE REST OF THE BALLS SHOULD BE EVENLY SPACED AROUND THE HOLE.

STARTING WITH THE 12 O'CLOCK-PLACED BALL, SET THE PUTTER HEAD BEHIND AND GENTLY TOUCH THE BALL. NOW, WITH A GOOD PUTTING STANCE AND WITHOUT TAKING A BACKSWING, "PUSH" THE BALL INTO THE HOLE. CONTINUE AROUND THE "CLOCK" UNTIL YOU HAVE PUSHED ALL THE BALLS. SCORE YOUR MADE PUTTS AS FOLLOWS:

> 12, 3, 6, & 9 O'CLOCK BALLS = 1 PT. EACH
> ALL THE OTHERS= 2 PTS. EACH

IF YOU CAN "PUSH IN" MORE THAN 16 POINTS YOU ARE GETTING THE HANG OF IT!!! TRY FOR 18 POINTS, THEN 20 !

"PUSH N' TIME" WILL HELP YOU TO ACCELERATE THROUGH YOUR PUTTS, INSTEAD OF STOPPING OR JABBING AT THEM. PLUS IT WILL IMPROVE YOUR ABILITY TO SWING YOUR PUTTER ON YOUR INTENDED LINE.

DANNY MULHEARN, PGA
GLEN OAK COUNTRY CLUB
630.469.5600

Notes

THE WINDMILL

"THE WINDMILL" WILL IMPROVE YOUR FOCUS AND CONCENTRATION ON SHORT PUTTS.

CREATE FOUR LINES OF FIVE BALLS MOVING OUT IN FOUR OPPOSITE DIRECTIONS FROM THE HOLE ON THE PUTTING GREEN. (CONFUSED? WELL, THINK OF THE ARMS OF A WINDMILL.) ALLOW A ONE FOOT INTERVAL BETWEEN EACH BALL.

THE OBJECT OF THE GAME IS TO SINK ALL OF THE PUTTS OF EACH "ARM," IN A ROW, STARTING WITH THE CLOSEST AND MOVING OUT TO THE FARTHEST. THE FIRST PUTT IS WORTH ONE STROKE, THE SECOND TWO, THROUGH TO THE FIFTH, BEING WORTH 5 STROKES. IF YOU CAN SINK AN ENTIRE "ARM" IT COUNTS AS 15 STROKES. PAR FOR THE ENTIRE "WINDMILL" IS 60. IF YOU ARE ABLE TO MAKE ALL FIVE OF AN ARM, WITHOUT A MISS, YOU MAY SUBTRACT ONE STROKE FROM THAT "ARM" TOTAL, FOR A 14. HOWEVER, IF YOU MISS ANY OF THE PUTTS IN AN "ARM," YOU MUST ADD A PENALTY STROKE AND BEGIN THAT "ARM" OVER. ONCE YOU COMPLETE AN "ARM" CONTINUE ON TO THE NEXT.

SHOOTING "THE WINDMILL" BELOW PAR IS THE GOAL, BUT IT TAKES MUCH PRACTICE AND PATIENCE!

THE SHORT ONE TO FIVE FOOT PUTTS ARE CRUCIAL IN ORDER TO POST A GOOD SCORE. "THE WINDMILL" OFFERS YOU THE OPPORTUNITY TO SHARPEN YOUR FOCUS AND SIGNIFICANTLY INCREASE YOUR CONFIDENCE TO DRAIN THE SHORT ONES CONSISTENTLY.

PENNI GODDEN, LPGA
KLEIN CREEK GOLF CLUB
630.690.0101

Notes

18 IN A ROW

"18 IN A ROW" WILL HELP YOU TO BUILD YOUR CONFIDENCE IN MAKING YOUR SHORT PUTTS.

THE OBJECT OF THE GAME IS TO MAKE 18 THREE FOOT PUTTS IN A ROW. BREAK THE PUTTS INTO 3 GROUPS OF 6 PUTTS. EACH GROUP OF PUTTS SHOULD COME AT THE HOLE FROM A DIFFERENT ANGLE. PUTTS 1 THROUGH 5 FOR EACH GROUP ARE WORTH ONE POINT, WITH THE SIXTH, THE LAST PUTT, BEING WORTH 2 POINTS. SO, EACH GROUP IS WORTH 7 POINTS. THE TOTAL POINTS FOR THE ENTIRE GAME IS 21. IF, AT ANY POINT A PUTT IS MISSED, YOU MUST START OVER.

CAN YOU GET TO 21 POINTS? IF NOT, TRY TO GET TO 18, OR 15, OR 12. REMEMBER, IT IS ABOUT DOING <u>YOUR</u> BEST!

IF YOU GET GOOD AT MAKING EIGHTEEN THREEFOOT-ERS, TRY MOVING TO FIVE, THEN SEVEN FEET.

GOOD LUCK !!!

DON'T RUSH THROUGH "18 IN A ROW." THE GOAL IS TO MAKE THE PUTTS, NOT TO MAKE THEM QUICKLY. I RECOMMEND THAT YOU GO THROUGH YOUR FULL PRE-SHOT ROUTINE FOR EACH ATTEMPT. AFTER ALL, YOU WILL USE YOUR ROUTINE OUT ON THE COURSE, RIGHT? UNDER PRESSURE YOU WILL REVERT TO THAT SAME ROUTINE IF YOU DO IT EACH TIME.

MICHAEL JONES
CANTIGNY GOLF CLUB
630.668.3323

Notes

 # PULL-BACK PUTTING

 "PULL-BACK PUTTING" WILL HELP YOU TO BE VERY AWARE OF THE STROKE NECESSARY TO LEAVE YOUR LONGER PUTTS CLOSER TO THE HOLE.

THIS GAME CAN BE PLAYED BY YOURSELF OR CAN BE PLAYED COMPETITIVELY WITH A PLAYING PARTNER. YOU ONLY NEED ONE BALL AND YOUR PUTTER TO PLAY.

THROUGHOUT THE GAME, YOU SELECT THE PUTT YOU ARE TRYING TO MAKE. ALL PUTTS MUST BE GREATER THAN 15 FEET IN DISTANCE. PICK A CUP TO PUTT TO, AND USING YOUR FULL PUTTING ROUTINE, ATTEMPT TO MAKE THE PUTT. IF YOU AREN'T SUCCESSFUL, YOU HAVE TWO CHOICES: ONE, PUTT FROM THE SPOT WHERE THE FIRST PUTT STOPPED, OR TWO, PULL-BACK THE BALL ONE PUTTER LENGTH AND ATTEMPT AGAIN FROM THE NEW SPOT. YOU ARE ONLY ALLOWED TWO PUTTS PER HOLE.

SCORING

3 POINTS... MAKE YOUR FIRST PUTT
1 POINT... MAKE YOUR SECOND PUTT
2 POINTS... MAKE YOUR "PULL-BACK" PUTT
-1 POINT... MISS YOUR "PULL-BACK" PUTT

PLAY 9 OR 18 HOLES OF "PULL-BACK PUTTING." THE PLAYER WITH THE MOST POINTS WINS! OR, IF YOU ARE PLAYING ALONE, GO FOR A CERTAIN GOAL SCORE !!!

 BE AWARE OF YOUR FIRST PUTTS... ARE YOU CONSISTENTLY LEAVING THEM SHORT, LEFT, RIGHT, OR LONG? BE READY TO MAKE ADJUSTMENTS.

 MARALEE MALANEY, LPGA MEDINAH COUNTRY CLUB 630.773.1702

Notes

CHIPPING

WHACK!

 **21**

 YOU WILL NEED A PLAYING PARTNER FOR THIS GAME. YOU CAN EVEN PLAY WITH THREE OR FOUR PLAYERS!!!

THE PLAYER WHO IS CLOSEST TO THE AGE OF 21 GETS TO GO FIRST. THE REST CAN FOLLOW IN ANY ORDER YOU WISH. PLAYER "A" CHIPS A BALL FROM ANYWHERE AROUND THE GREEN (OR IN A BUNKER) TO A PIN OF HIS CHOICE WITH A CLUB OF HIS CHOICE. THEN, THE OTHER PLAYER(S) ATTEMPT TO CHIP FROM THE SAME SPOT, USING A DIFFERENT CLUB, AND TRY TO GET CLOSER TO THE PIN. ROTATE WHO GOES FIRST AFTER EACH POINT.

SCORING 21 GOES LIKE THIS: THE PLAYER THAT IS CLOSEST TO THE PIN GETS 1 POINT. IF A PLAYER CHIPS IT IN, HE GETS 3 POINTS. IF YOU ARE PLAYING WITH MORE THAN TWO PLAYERS, THE PLAYER THAT IS FARTHEST FROM THE PIN MUST SUBTRACT 1 POINT. THE FIRST PLAYER TO 21 WINS !!!

 IT IS IMPORTANT TO FOLLOW THE BALL ALL OF THE WAY TO WHERE IT STOPS ROLLING. BY FOLLOWING THE CHIP TO ITS STOPPING POINT A PLAYER CAN GAIN IMPORTANT KNOWLEDGE OF THE ROLL OF THE GREEN.

STAY POSITIVE!!!

 DAN KOCHEVAR, PGA
OAK BROOK GOLF COURSE
630.990.3032

Notes

 **5-10-15-20**

 DROP 5 BALLS A FEW FEET FROM THE EDGE OF THE GREEN. CHIP EACH BALL TO A PIN OF YOUR CHOICE. THEN, GO ON AND TRY TO MAKE ALL FIVE PUTTS FOR A SUCCESSFUL "UP & DOWN." IF YOU ARE SUCCESSFUL WITH FIVE BALLS, THEN YOU CAN MOVE UP TO 10 BALLS. IF YOU CAN CHIP AND PUTT- IN ALL 10 BALLS, THEN YOU CAN MOVE UP TO 15 BALLS, AND THEN TO 20.

REMEMBER, IF YOU MISS A PUTT AT ANY LEVEL, YOU MUST START OVER AT THE BEGINNING OF THAT LEVEL. THIS IS A GREAT GAME FOR NOVICES TO TOURING PROS. 5-10-15-20 WILL CERTAINLY IMPROVE YOUR GREENSIDE TOUCH AND CONFIDENCE.

PRACTICE LIKE A PRO !!!

 FOR GREENSIDE CHIPS, CHOKE DOWN A LITTLE ON THE CLUB THAT YOU ARE USING. IT IS BEST TO AVOID USING YOUR WRISTS; INSTEAD USE A PUTTING-STYLE STROKE. ALWAYS REMEMBER, "HIT DOWN AND YOU WILL NOT FROWN."

 DR. JIM SUTTIE, PGA
DR. JIM SUTTIE GOLF ACADEMY
1.800.765.3838

Notes

 **Recipe** # ADD IT UP

 **Ingredients**

TAKE TEN BALLS AND SCATTER THEM AROUND ABOUT FIVE FEET OFF OF THE EDGE OF THE GREEN. THE BALLS DON'T NEED TO BE IN ANY PARTICULAR ORDER, BUT ONCE THEY LAND THIS IS THE EXACT LIE THAT YOU MUST CHIP EACH OF THEM FROM. CHIP EACH BALL TO A HOLE OF YOUR CHOICE. THE CLOSER THE HOLE THAT YOU CHOOSE THE EASIER "ADD IT UP" WILL BE. FOR YOU PROS, CHOOSE A HOLE FURTHER WAY. AFTER YOU HAVE CHIPPED EACH BALL, MEASURE THE DISTANCE EACH BALL IS FROM THE HOLE. (THE SIMPLEST WAY IS TO STEP-OFF THE DISTANCE BY GOING HEEL-TO-TOE) THEN, SIMPLY ADD UP THE TOTAL DISTANCE FOR ALL TEN CHIPS. REPEAT "ADD IT UP!" THREE TIMES AND SEE IF YOU CAN REDUCE THE TOTAL DISTANCE FROM THE PREVIOUS ATTEMPT.

IF YOU CAN CHIP ALL TEN BALLS AND REDUCE YOUR TOTAL DISTANCE FIVE TIMES IN A ROW, YOU ARE REALLY GETTING BETTER!

 **Tips**

THE LENGTH OF THE BACKSWING IS VERY IMPORTANT IN CHIPPING. FOR LONGER CHIPS BRING YOUR HANDS BACK TO THE TEN O'CLOCK POSITION, BUT FOR SHORTER CHIPS ONLY TO THE SEVEN OR EIGHT O'CLOCK POSITION.

 **Chef**

RENIE CALKIN, LPGA
PRAIRIE LANDING GOLF CLUB
630.208.7600

Notes

 **BALOGNE SANDWICH**

 STAND YOUR GOLF BAG AT THE EDGE OF THE GREEN. (THIS GAME PLAYS THE BEST WITH A STAND BAG.) TAKE YOUR MOST LOFTED CLUB AND WALK AWAY FROM THE GREEN ABOUT TEN FEET, KEEPING THE BAG BETWEEN YOU AND THE GREEN. THEN DROP THREE BALLS IN THE GRASS. PITCH YOUR FIRST BALL TOWARD THE BAG, INTENDING TO JUST BARELY CLEAR THE TOP OF THE BAG AND HAVE THE BALL LAND ON THE GREEN. MARK THE SPOT WHERE IT LANDS BY LAYING A CLUB DOWN PERPENDICULAR TO THE FLIGHT PATH OF THE BALL. THIS FIRST CLUB REPRESENTS THE TOP LAYER OF BREAD IN A BALOGNE SANDWICH. NOW, RETURN TO YOUR PITCHING SPOT. REPEAT THE PREVIOUS STEP, INCLUDING LAYING ANOTHER CLUB ON THE GREEN. THIS SECOND CLUB REPRESENTS THE BOTTOM LAYER OF BREAD ON A BALOGNE SANDWICH. NOW, COMES THE BALOGNE!

PITCH YOUR THIRD BALL TRYING TO HAVE IT LAND BETWEEN THE "BREAD" (THE CLUBS) TO COMPLETE YOUR BALOGNE SANDWICH. IF YOU CAN PLACE YOUR BALOGNE PROPERLY 3 OUT OF 5 TRIES, YOU ARE QUITE A CHEF!

 THIS GAME WILL HELP YOU DEVELOP THE FEEL FOR A HIGH, LOFTED SHOT AND WILL ADD A SENSE OF PRESSURE TO THE "BALOGNE" SHOT. I RECOMMEND THAT YOUR BACK SWING MATCHES THE LENGTH OF YOUR FOLLOW-THROUGH. THIS IS A TOUGH GAME... NO BALOGNE!

 JOHN CRAIG, PGA
CRYSTAL WOODS GOLF COURSE
815.338.3111

Notes

 **BOGEY**

YEP! YOU GUESSED IT. THIS A DIRECT KNOCK-OFF OF THE GREATEST DRIVEWAY BASKETBALL GAME EVER... HORSE. AS YOU KNOW, YOU WILL NEED A PLAYING PARTNER FOR "BOGEY."

PLAYER ONE DECLARES THE SHOT AND CLUB THAT HE IS GOING TO HIT. FOR EXAMPLE, A FLOP SHOT OVER A BUNKER WITH A SAND WEDGE, OR A BUMP AND RUN OUT OF THICK CUT WITH A 3 WOOD, AND THE LIKE. AFTER PLAYER ONE HITS THE "DECLARED" SHOT, THEN THE REST OF THE PLAYERS HAVE TO FOLLOW SUIT. AFTER ALL OF THE PLAYERS HAVE HIT THE "DECLARED" SHOT, THEY ALL MUST ATTEMPT TO ONE-PUTT OUT.

ANYONE THAT CAN'T ONE PUTT, INCLUDING THE PLAYER THAT "DECLARED" THE SHOT, GETS A LETTER "B." IF A PLAYER CAN ONE-PUTT, HE AVOIDS GETTING A LETTER. CONTINUE ROTATING WHICH PLAYER "DECLARES" UNTIL ALL BUT ONE PLAYER IS LEFT WITHOUT THE WORD "B-O-G-E-Y." IF A PLAYER HITS THE "DECLARED" SHOT INTO THE HOLE, ALL OTHER PLAYERS GET A LETTER.

"BOGEY" REALLY HELPS PLAYERS TO BECOME MORE CREATIVE AROUND THE GREEN AND REQUIRES THAT THEY TRY DIFFERENT CLUBS. AFTER ALL, SOMEDAY YOU MIGHT HAVE TO HIT A CREATIVE SHOT TO SAVE A PAR !

CRAIG CARNEY
MEDINAH COUNTRY CLUB
630.773.1300

Notes

 **CHIPPETY-DOO-DAH**

 PICK FOUR SPOTS AROUND THE PRACTICE GREEN THAT HAVE FOUR DISTINCTLY DIFFERENT LIES. FOR EXAMPLE, DOWN-HILL, UPHILL, HARD PAN, THICK GRASS, SHORT GRASS, IN A DIVOT, ETC. REMEMBER, THE MORE DIFFICULT LIES THAT YOU CHOOSE THE MORE YOU WILL IM-PROVE YOUR SHORT GAME. MARK EACH OF THESE SPOTS WITH A BALL STICK, TOWEL, OR THE LIKE. YOU NEED NOT PLACE A BALL AT THESE SPOTS, AS YOU WILL USE THE SAME BALL THROUGHOUT "CHIPPETY-DO-DAH."

THE OBJECT OF "CHIPPETY-DOO-DAH" IS TO COMPLETE ALL FOUR HOLES IN AS FEW STROKES AS POSSIBLE, INCLUDING PUTTING OUT. IF YOU EXCEED 12 STROKES AT ANY POINT YOU MUST START OVER.

SCORING: 6-7 STROKES IS AWESOME!
             8-9 STROKES IS VERY GOOD.
             10-11 STROKES IS PRETTY GOOD.
             12 OR MORE... LOTS OF ROOM TO IMPROVE!

REMEMBER, DO <u>YOUR</u> BEST TO IMPROVE TO <u>YOUR</u> BEST!

 TO BECOME GREAT WITH YOUR SHORT GAME YOU HAVE TO TRUST WHAT YOU ARE DO-ING. "CHIPPETY-DOO-DAH" WILL PUT YOU IN "COURSE-LIKE" SITUATIONS THAT WILL CHALLENGE YOU AND, ULTIMATELY, HELP YOU TO TRUST YOUR SHORT GAME.

ENJOY!

 BETTY KAUFMAN, LPGA
PINE MEADOW GOLF CLUB
847.566.4653

Notes

On Memory

IMAGINE YOUR MEMORY IS A JAR FULL OF JELLYBEANS.
IN YOUR JAR THERE ARE ONLY TWO FLAVORS OF BEANS:
CHERRY RED AND LIME GREEN.
EACH CHERRY RED BEAN IS A MEMORY OF A GOLF
SHOT THAT YOU HAVE CHOSEN TO PLACE IN YOUR JAR
THAT WAS FRUSTRATING, UGLY, AND DISAPPOINTING.
EACH LIME GREEN BEAN IS A MEMORY OF A GOLF SHOT
THAT YOU HAVE CHOSEN TO PLACE IN YOUR JAR
THAT WAS WELL-STRUCK, SMOOTH, AND
A SOURCE OF ENORMOUS PRIDE.
NOW, IF YOU CLOSED YOUR EYES AND GRABBED A
RANDOM BEAN OUT OF YOUR JELLY BEAN MEMORY JAR,
WOULD IT MORE LIKELY BE CHERRY RED OR LIME GREEN?
YOUR MEMORY IS YOUR CHOICE.

Notes

 **CLOSE IT OUT**

 YOU PLAY FIVE SHOTS CHIPPED FROM FIVE DIFFERENT LOCATIONS AROUND THE PRACTICE PUTTING GREEN. IF POSSIBLE, ONE OF THE SPOTS SHOULD BE IN A BUNKER. THE OBJECT IS TO RACK UP AS MANY POINTS AS POSSIBLE WITH YOUR FIVE BALLS.

EACH BALL IS CHIPPED TO A PIN OF YOUR CHOICE. BE SURE TO VARY THE PINS FOR DISTANCE AND DIFFICULTY.

SCORING FOR THE CHIP:

> 2 POINTS, WITHIN ONE PUTTER LENGTH OF HOLE
> 3 POINTS, WITHIN ONE FOOT OF HOLE
> 5 POINTS FOR HOLED CHIP
> -1 POINT, OUTSIDE OF PUTTER LENGTH OF HOLE

SCORING FOR PUTTS:

> 2 POINTS FOR A MADE PUTT INSIDE OF ONE
>   PUTTER LENGTH
> 3 POINTS FOR A PUTT MADE OUTSIDE OF ONE
>   PUTTER LENGTH
> -1 POINT FOR A MISSED PUTT

"CLOSE IT OUT" IS ESPECIALLY FUN WITH A PARTNER!

 "CLOSE IT OUT" IS ALL ABOUT TRUSTING YOUR SHORT GAME AND CLOSING OUT THE HOLE!

DEVELOPING A SHARP AND CONSISTENT SHORT GAME IS CRUCIAL TO PLAYING GREAT GOLF. BE VERY AWARE OF HOW THE BALL REACTS TO THE GREEN WITH YOUR CHIPS AND BE ABLE TO MAKE NECESSARY ADJUSTMENTS WITH CLUB SELECTION.

 BILL ABRAMS, PGA
GOLF SOLUTIONS ACADEMY
708.727.0524

Notes

HIGH AND LOW

"HIGH AND LOW" WILL GREATLY IMPROVE YOUR FEEL FOR GREENSIDE PITCHES AND CHIPS.

CHOOSE YOUR GREENSIDE PITCHING CLUB. I LIKE TO USE MY SAND WEDGE. THEN, TAKE A SMALL DRIVING RANGE BUCKET AND PLACE IT ON THE EDGE OF THE PITCHING GREEN. GO TO A SPOT ABOUT 20 FEET FROM THE BASKET AND DROP ABOUT TWENTY BALLS. THE FARTHER THAT YOU DROP THE BALLS FROM THE BASKET, THE MORE DIFFICULT THAT "HIGH AND LOW" WILL BE.

NOW, ALTERNATE HITTING A HIGH PITCH SHOT AND A LOW CHIP SHOT TRYING TO GET ONE TYPE OF EACH SHOT IN THE BASKET. KEEP TRACK OF HOW MANY PITCHES IT TAKES YOU TO GET ONE HIGH AND ONE LOW IN THE BASKET.

TO MAKE "HIGH AND LOW" EVEN MORE CHALLENGING, MOVE FARTHER AWAY FROM THE BASKET. FOR A REAL CHALLENGE, TRY TO GET ONE HIGH PITCH SHOT AND ONE LOW CHIP SHOT IN THE BASKET ON BACK-TO-BACK SHOTS.

WITH BOTH HIGH AND LOW SHOTS, IT IS IMPORTANT TO MAINTAIN A SECURE, YET DELICATE GRIP ON YOUR CLUB. FOR YOUR LOW PITCH SHOTS, PLACE THE BALL FURTHER BACK IN YOUR STANCE AND FOR HIGH PITCH SHOTS MOVE THE BALL TOWARD THE FRONT OF YOUR STANCE. GET THE "FEELING" AND HAVE FUN !

BILLY KLEMZ, PGA
ARROWHEAD GOLF CLUB
630.653.5800

Notes

 **MONEY BALL**

 "MONEY BALL" IS MODELED AFTER THE 3 POINT CONTEST AT THE NBA ALL-STAR GAME. "MONEY BALL" CAN BE PLAYED WITH TWO OR MORE PLAYERS.

OBJECT: CHIP THE BALL IN THE HOLE. PERIOD!

CHIP FIVE CONSECUTIVE BALLS FROM A SPOT A COUPLE FEET OFF OF THE EDGE OF THE GREEN. CHIPS 1 THROUGH 4 ARE EACH WORTH 1 POINT, AND THE FIFTH CHIP, THE "MONEY BALL," IS WORTH A WHOPPING 5 POINTS! AFTER FIVE CHIPS FROM ONE SPOT, MOVE TO ANOTHER SPOT. REPEAT THIS FIVE TIMES AND TOTAL YOUR SCORE.

5-7 POINTS...	IT'S A LONG ROAD TO AUGUSTA!
8-12 POINTS...	GONNA BE A STAR SOMEDAY !
13-15 POINTS...	SHARPSHOOTER!
16-20 POINTS...	TIGER JR.
20 OR MORE...	SHORT GAME GAMER!

 BEING REALLY EFFECTIVE WITH YOUR SHORT GAME MEANS GETTING OUT OF THE MECHANICS AND LETTING YOUR "FEEL" TAKE OVER. SO, BE SURE TO "SEE" THE SHOT YOU ARE ATTEMPTING BEFORE YOU DO IT, THEN SHUT YOUR BRAIN OFF AND "LET IT HAPPEN."

 JOHN SWAN, PGA
FOX BEND GOLF COURSE
847.712.4640

Notes

ODD CLUB OUT

GRAB 2 OR 3 CLUBS OUT OF YOUR BAG THAT YOU NORMALLY WOULDN'T USE FOR CHIPPING, SUCH AS A 5 WOOD AND A 4 IRON. THEN, DROP 5 BALLS AROUND THE EDGE OF THE GREEN. NOW COMES THE FUN PART.

WITH THE "ODD" CLUBS AND YOUR PUTTER, TAKE THE FIVE BALLS AND TRY TO GET UP & DOWN WITH EACH BALL. CHIP AND THEN PUTT EACH BALL... DON'T CHIP FIVE IN A ROW AND THEN PUT FIVE IN A ROW. REMEMBER, PRACTICE IS FOR LEARNING HOW TO PLAY BETTER OUT ON THE COURSE, AND YOU DON'T CHIP FIVE IN A ROW OUT ON THE COURSE, RIGHT?

SCORING GOES LIKE THIS:

    5 OUT OF 5... PGA PRO
    4 OUT OF 5... TOUR BOUND
    3 OUT OF 5... CLUB CHAMP
    FEWER THAN 3 OUT OF 5... PRACTICE TIME.

"FEEL" CANNOT BE TAUGHT, IT MUST BE LEARNED. USING "ODD" CLUBS AROUND THE GREEN DURING PRACTICE WILL IMPROVE YOUR FEEL AND ENHANCE YOUR IMAGINATION.

BE CREATIVE!

JOHN ESPOSITO, PGA
THE GOLF LEARNING CENTER
630.773.65677

Notes

ON THE EDGE

YOU WILL NEED ONE BALL AND NINE CLUBS TO COMPLETE A ROUND OF "ON THE EDGE." ALL OF YOUR CHIPS AND PITCHES WILL BE MORE THAN THREE FEET AND LESS THAN TEN FEET OFF OF THE EDGE OF THE GREEN.

START ANYWHERE AROUND THE CHIPPING GREEN YOU WISH. DROP A BALL , CHOOSE A CLUB, AND CHIP OR PITCH THAT BALL TO THE FURTHEST PIN FROM WHERE YOU ARE STANDING. YOU CAN ONLY USE A CLUB ONCE DURING A ROUND (NINE "HOLES"), SO CHOOSE YOUR CLUB WISELY BASED UPON THE DISTANCE TO THE HOLE OR THE TYPE, OR THICKNESS, OF THE GRASS. NOW, PUTT OUT THIS CHIP AND KEEP TRACK OF THE NUMBER OF STROKES. ROTATE CLOCKWISE AROUND THE GREEN FOR EACH SUCCESSIVE CHIP OR PITCH, ALL THE WHILE ADDING UP YOUR STROKES AND REMEMBERING NOT TO USE A CLUB MORE THAN ONCE (EXCEPT FOR YOUR PUTTER, OF COURSE). YOUR NINTH "HOLE" SHOULD BRING YOU BACK TO THE AREA OF YOUR FIRST CHIP. 18 IS PAR FOR THE COURSE.

A GREAT SCORE IS UNDER PAR !

TO INCREASE THE DIFFICULTY OF "ON THE EDGE," YOU CAN EXTEND YOUR "EDGE" TO 15 FEET OFF OF THE GREEN. IT WILL FEEL STRANGE TO USE A 3 IRON OR A WOOD TO CHIP, BUT YOUR SHOT-MAKING ABILITY WILL IMPROVE DRAMATICALLY IF YOU PRACTICE "ON THE EDGE."

MARGIE MUZIK, LPGA
ST. CHARLES COUNTRY CLUB
630.377.9340

Notes

 **Recipe**

REALITY CHECK

 **Ingredients**

YOU CAN PLAY "REALITY CHECK" BY YOURSELF OR WITH A PARTNER.

SELECT THREE HOLES ON THE PRACTICE GREEN THAT WILL ALLOW, FROM THE SAME SPOT, A PITCH (SAND WEDGE), A CHIP (9 IRON), AND A BUMP AND RUN (7 IRON). DROP THREE BALLS AT THAT SPOT.

THE OBJECT OF THE GAME IS TO PITCH, CHIP, AND BUMP & RUN EACH OF THE BALLS TO THEIR RESPECTIVE HOLE <u>AND</u> PUTT THEM OUT FOR A SCORE OF TWO. PAR FOR THE ROUND (THREE BALLS) WOULD BE A SIX.

SEE HOW MANY "ROUNDS" IT TAKES YOU TO GET UNDER PAR! TRY 3, 6, OR 9 ROUNDS AND ADD UP YOUR SCORES. THIS GAME SIMULATES THE PRESSURE YOU WILL FEEL TO GET UP & DOWN ON THE COURSE... THUS, A REALITY CHECK!

HAVE FUN !!!

 **Tips**

THE BEST WAY TO PRACTICE IS TO CREATE THE FEELING OF PRESSURE THAT YOU WILL FEEL IN A COMPETITIVE ROUND. AVOID JUST PRACTICING FOR THE SAKE OF PRACTICING... MAKE IT REAL.

 **Chef**

PRESTON IRWIN, PGA
SCHAUMBURG GOLF CLUB
847.885.9000

Notes

On Patience

SHOT BY SHOT. HOLE BY HOLE.
ROUND BY ROUND. SEASON BY SEASON.
AND SO IT GOES. ALL TOO OFTEN, PLAYERS
GET FAR AHEAD OF THEMSELVES AS THEY
APPROACH THEIR GOLF LIVES. THE REAL CHALLENGE
ISN'T CRAFTING A GREAT GOLF CAREER, THE REAL
CHALLENGE IS CRAFTING A GREAT GOLF SHOT...
...AND LETTING THE CAREER TAKE CARE OF ITSELF.

Notes

SLIPPERY SLOPE

"SLIPPERY SLOPE" IS ALL ABOUT DEVELOPING BETTER FEEL AND CONFIDENCE FOR YOUR DOWNHILL CHIPS.

SET TEN BALLS OFF OF THE EDGE, ON THE HIGH SIDE, OF THE PRACTICE GREEN. THEN, SET A CLUB HEAD COVER ON THE GREEN WHERE THE DOWN-SLOPE STOPS. THE MORE SLOPE, THE GREATER THE DIFFICULTY OF THIS GAME. CHIP YOUR FIRST BALL TRYING TO HAVE IT STOP WITHIN 3 FEET OF YOUR CLUB HEAD COVER. THIS IS YOUR "OPENER." SO YOU CAN'T CONTINUE UNTIL YOU ARE SUCCESSFUL. ONCE YOU HAVE "OPENED," NOW YOU ARE READY TO GO DOWN THE "SLIPPERY SLOPE."

THE OBJECTIVE IS TO HAVE EACH SUCCESSIVE CHIP STOP SHORT OF THE PREVIOUS CHIP. SO, YOU ARE ACTUALLY WORKING YOUR WAY FROM YOUR "OPENER" CHIP TOWARD THE SPOT WHERE YOU ARE CHIPPING FROM.

YOUR FIRST CHIP IS WORTH 1 POINT, WITH EACH SUCCESSIVE CHIP WORTH ONE POINT MORE. SO, YOUR SECOND CHIP IS WORTH 2, ALL THE WAY TO YOUR NINTH CHIP, WHICH IS WORTH 9 POINTS. IF AT ANY POINT A CHIP ROLLS PAST THE PREVIOUS CHIP, YOU ARE THROUGH. ADD UP YOUR SCORE FOR YOUR SUCCESSFUL CHIPS. A PERFECT SCORE IS 45. HOW WELL CAN YOU CHIP DOWN THAT "SLIPPERY SLOPE?"

I PREFER THAT YOU CHANGE CLUBS DEPENDING UPON THE LENGTH OF THE CHIP. USE A LOWER CLUB (7 IRON) FOR A LONGER CHIP VERSUS A HIGHER CLUB (A WEDGE) FOR A SHORT CHIP.

TOM O'CONNOR, PGA
TOM O'CONNOR GOLF ACADEMY
815.557.3524

Notes

70

SOFTBALL

"SOFTBALL" IS A TWO-PLAYER CHIPPING GAME THAT IS SURE TO IMPROVE YOUR FEEL AND ENHANCE YOUR ABILITY TO UNDER-STAND THE LOFT AND CHARACTERISTICS OF DIFFERENT CLUBS.

EACH PLAYER WILL NEED 21 BALLS (THREE PER INNING) AND HIS 5, 6, 7, 8, 9, PITCHING AND SAND WEDGES. THE OBJECT IS OF "SOFTBALL" IS TO CHIP THE EACH BALL CLOSE TO THE HOLE TO SCORE RUNS AND WIN THE GAME.

CHIPPING FROM ABOUT 10 FEET OFF OF THE GREEN, PLAYER ONE CHIPS THREE BALLS WITH HIS 5 IRON AT A MUTUALLY DECIDED UPON HOLE. THEN, PLAYER TWO THEN FOLLOWS SUIT, ALSO WITH HIS 5 IRON. WALK TO THE BALLS AND SCORE THEM AS SUCH:

1 RUN...	WITHIN THREE FEET OF THE HOLE.
2 RUNS...	WITHIN TWO FEET OF THE HOLE.
3 RUNS...	WITHIN ONE FOOT OF THE HOLE.
GRAND SLAM...	IN THE HOLE !!!

ALTERNATE THE PLAYER CHIPPING ORDER EACH INNING AND ADVANCE TO THE NEXT CLUB EACH INNING, ENDING WITH THE SAND WEDGE.. IF BALLS CONTACT EACH OTHER AT ANY POINT, THEY WILL BE PLAYED AS THEY LIE. IF A TIE EXISTS AFTER SEVEN INNINGS, PLAY EXTRA INNINGS WITH YOUR 3 IRON.

CHIPPING WELL REQUIRES A FINE UNDERSTANDING OF THE CHARACTERISTICS OF EACH CLUB THAT IS USED. LEARN, BY PRACTICING AND PLAYING "SOFTBALL", JUST HOW THE BALL COMES OFF OF EACH CLUB. BE AWARE OF LOFT AND SPIN.

JIM KARRAS, PGA
WHISPER CREEK GOLF CLUB
847.515.7680

71

Notes

THE LADDER

PLACE A SMALL PILE OF BALLS A FEW FEET OFF OF THE EDGE OF THE GREEN. CHIP THE FIRST BALL JUST BARELY ON THE EDGE OF THE GREEN AND LET IT ROLL TO A STOP. THIS IS YOUR ALPHA BALL. . EACH CHIP, THEREAFTER, MUST EXCEED THE DISTANCE (INCLUDING THE ROLL, OF COURSE) OF THE PREVIOUS CHIP. THE GOAL IS TO SEE HOW MANY CHIPS YOU CAN MAKE BEFORE YOU HAVE ONE ROLL OFF THE OTHER SIDE OF THE GREEN. KEEP TRACK OF YOUR SCORES AND, AS ALWAYS, TRY TO IMPROVE AND BEAT YOUR PREVIOUS BEST.

"THE LADDER" GAME ALLOWS FOR MANY VARIATIONS. FOR EXAMPLE, TO MAKE IT MORE DIFFICULT, CHIP ON A DOWNHILL GREEN. TRY USING DIFFERENT CLUBS TO IMPROVE YOUR CONFIDENCE AND FEEL AROUND THE GREEN.

THIS IS A GREAT GAME TO PLAY WITH A PARTNER ! PARTNER, TOO !!

GAMES ARE A GREAT WAY TO HAVE FUN AND IMPROVE YOUR OVERALL GREENSIDE FEEL . IT IS BEST, ULTIMATELY, NOT TO WORRY SO MUCH ABOUT THE OUTCOME OF THE SHOT. INSTEAD, FOCUS ON THE FEEL OF THE SHOT. IMPROVING IN GOLF IS A LOT LIKE CLIMBING A LADDER... ONE STEP AT A TIME.

CONNIE DEMATTIA, PGA
MEDINAH COUNTRY CLUB
630.773.1700

Notes

THE LIMBO

DON'T WORRY, DESPITE ITS NAME, "THE LIMBO" WON'T ADD ANY LUMBAR STRESS TO YOU PLAYERS WITH FRAGILE BACKS!

FIRST, ON A PRACTICE CHIPPING GREEN, CREATE A FIVE FOOT CIRCLE AROUND A HOLE USING SPARE TEES.. NEXT, PLACE ABOUT FIFTEEN BALLS 10-15 FEET OFF OF THE EDGE OF THE GREEN. NOW, BETWEEN THE PILE OF BALLS AND THE HOLE, AND OFF OF THE GREEN, SET UP A LIMBO-STYLE BAR POLE ABOUT 3 FEET HIGH. (YOU COULD DO THIS WITH A GOLF CLUB SET ACROSS TWO STANDING GOLF BAGS.)

OBJECT: TO CHIP OR PITCH THE BALL EITHER OVER OR UNDER THE LIMBO POLE AND HAVE IT STOP WITHIN THE CIRCLE OF TEES ON THE GREEN.

SCORING: 2 POINTS FOR SUCCESSFULLY HITTING YOUR "CALL" SHOT (EITHER OVER OR UNDER) AND LANDING INSIDE THE CIRCLE.

-1 POINT IF YOU MISS, IN ANY WAY, YOUR "CALL" SHOT (NOT OVER, NOT UNDER, OR IF IT DOES NOT IN LAND CIRCLE, ETC.)

5 POINTS IF YOU HIT YOUR "CALL" SHOT AND HOLE OUT.

SEE HOW MANY POINTS YOU CAN SCORE USING 15 BALLS AND TRY TO BEAT YOUR BEST SCORE. "THE LIMBO" IS GREAT TO PLAY WITH A PARTNER.

YOU MUST CALL "OVER" OR "UNDER" BEFORE YOU HIT. I USUALLY ATTEMPT FIFTEEN OVER, THEN FIFTEEN UNDER IN A ROW.. BUT, DO AS YOU PLEASE.

BILL BROLLEY, PGA
STEEPLE CHASE GOLF CLUB
847.949.8900

Notes

 # UP & OVER

"UP & OVER" IS A
CHIPPING OR PITCHING
GAME THAT CAN BE PLAYED
ANYWHERE.

PLACE YOUR GOLF BAG IN A SPOT WHERE THERE AREN'T
MANY OTHER PLAYERS AROUND. ("UP & OVER" WORKS
BEST IF YOU HAVE A SELF-STANDING TYPE BAG.)
STEP-OFF FIVE PACES MOVING AWAY IN ANY DIRECTION
FROM YOUR BAG AND PLACE A SMALL (ABOUT 2'X2')
TOWEL ON THE GROUND. CONTINUE FIVE MORE PACES IN
THE SAME DIRECTION AND PLACE ANOTHER TOWEL ON
THE GROUND. AND, ONCE AGAIN, FIVE MORE PACES AND
PLACE A THIRD TOWEL ON THE GROUND. GO TO A SPOT 5
FEET ON THE OPPOSITE SIDE OF THE BAG FROM THE
TOWELS DROP A SMALL PILE OF BALLS.
NOW, THE FUN BEGINS.

WITH A WEDGE, PITCH THE GOLF BALLS OVER YOUR BAG
AND TRY TO HAVE THEM LAND ON EACH OF THE TOWELS.
ALTERNATING BETWEEN THE THREE DIFFERENT
TOWELS AS TARGETS, TRY TO LAND 3, THEN 5, THEN 7 OF
THE 10 BALLS ON THE TOWELS.

"UP & OVER" WILL HELP YOU TO
GET A BALL IN THE AIR QUICKLY,
YET HAVE IT LAND SOFTLY... LIKE
OVER A BUNKER OR A BUSH ON
THE COURSE. TO GET THE BALL
UP FAST DO NOT "SCOOP" UNDER IT. INSTEAD, OPEN
YOUR STANCE, OPEN YOU CLUB FACE, AND SWING ACROSS
THE LINE OF THE TARGET.

SWOOOSH!

DENNIS JOHNSEN, PGA
PHEASANT RUN RESORT
630.584.4914

Notes

Bunkers Etc.

 **CHAOS**

"CHAOS" ISN'T REALLY CHAOS, IT JUST STARTS OUT THAT WAY!

PICK A SPOT ANYWHERE, OFF THE GREEN, AROUND THE PRACTICE GREEN AREA. TAKE FIVE BALLS AND TOSS THEM BACKWARDS OVER YOUR HEAD (MAKE SURE THAT NO ONE IS IN RANGE) AND LET THEM LAND WHERE THEY MAY. THE OBJECTIVE IS TO GET UP & DOWN FROM THESE CHAOTIC BALL LOCATIONS. SCORING GOES AS FOLLOWS:

> 10 POINTS... IF THE CHIP, PITCH, OR SAND SHOT LANDS WITHIN 1 CLUB LENGTH OF THE HOLE.
> 5 POINTS... IF THE CHIP, PITCH, OR SAND SHOT LANDS WITHIN 2 CLUB LENGTHS OF THE HOLE.
> -5 POINTS.. IF THE PLAYER FAILS TO REACH THE GREEN WITH HIS FIRST SHOT.

NOW THAT THE BALLS ARE ON THE GREEN IT IS TIME TO PUTT. SCORING GOES AS FOLLOWS:

> 10 POINTS... ONE PUTT.
> 5 POINTS... TWO PUTTS.
> -5 POINTS... THREE OR MORE PUTTS.

A PERFECT SCORE WOULD BE 100. SEE HOW CLOSE YOU CAN COME TO PERFECT. 90? 80? GOOD LUCK !!!

FOR A MORE ADVANCED FORM OF "CHAOS", PULL THE FIRST PUTT BACK ONE PUTTER LENGTH. THIS MAKES "CHAOS" EVEN MORE CHAOTIC. THIS IS A GREAT TEAM COMPETITION, ALSO.

TOM EVERS, PGA
PLUM TREE NATIONAL GOLF CLUB
815.943.7474

Notes

IMPOSSIBLE

Ingredients

WELL, MAYBE IT'S NOT IMPOSSIBLE, BUT IT IS VERY, VERY, VERY DIFFICULT. !!!

"IMPOSSIBLE" IS A FANTASTIC PITCHING AND CHIPPING (AND IF YOU ARE A GLUTTON FOR PUNISHMENT, YOU COULD PLAY OUT OF THE BUNKER, TOO) GAME THAT WILL TEST YOUR SKILLS AND YOUR PATIENCE.

THE OBJECT OF "IMPOSSIBLE" IS TO PITCH OR CHIP 6 BALLS, FROM OFF OF THE GREEN AND PUTT OUT TAKING 11 TOTAL STROKES, OR LESS.

PLACE 6 BALLS OFF OF THE GREEN AND PITCH OR CHIP, DEPENDING UPON WHICH CUP YOU SELECT, US-ING A SAND WEDGE, A PITCHING WEDGE, A 9, 8, 7, AND 6 IRON. YOU MUST USE EACH CLUB ONCE! FOLLOWING YOUR PITCH OR CHIP, THEN YOU PUTT EACH BALL OUT. MATHEMATICALLY, "IMPOSSIBLE" REQUIRES THAT YOU HOLE ONE OF YOUR CHIPS OR PITCHES AND ONE-PUTT THE REST. IF YOU EXCEED 11 POINTS, STOP, AND START OVER.

SEE HOW MANY ROUNDS IT TAKES TO WIN "IMPOSSIBLE," THEN TRY TO BEAT YOUR BEST SCORE.

IF YOU BECOME MENTALLY FATIGUED OR FRUSTRATED PLAYING "IMPOSSIBLE"... WELCOME TO THE CLUB ! JUST RELAX AND STAY FOCUSED.

DAVE O'NEAL PGA
THE ROYAL FOX COUNTRY CLUB
847.381.6884

Notes

BUNKER BONGO

THIS BUNKER GAME IS SIMPLE, YET FUN FOR PLAYERS OF ALL LEVELS. "BUNKER BONGO" IS MOST FUN WITH A PLAYING PART-NER, BUT PLAYS JUST FINE BY YOURSELF.

EACH PLAYER PLAYS ONE SHOT OUT OF THE BUNKER. THE CLOSEST BALL TO THE HOLE GETS ONE POINT. IF YOU HOLE IT OUT, YOU GET 3 POINTS! THE FIRST PLAYER TO REACH 15 POINTS WINS.

YOU COULD ALSO ASSIGN VARIOUS POINT VALUES (BEFORE THE SHOT IS PLAYED!) DEPENDING UPON THE DIFFICULTY LEVEL OF THE SHOT. IF YOU DO NOT HAVE A PLAYING PARTNER, GET "BUNKER BONGO'D" BY YOURSELF!

DEPENDING ON YOUR ABILITY LEVEL AND THE DIFFICULTY OF THE SHOT, GIVE YOURSELF A POINT IF YOU:

       1) GET IT OUT.
       2) GET IT ON.
       3) GET IT ON THE SAME SIDE OF THE GREEN AS
          THE FLAG.
       4) GET IT CLOSE

       AND , GIVE YOURSELF 3 POINTS IF YOU HOLE IT
       OUT !!! PLAY TO FIFTEEN.

COMMIT TO THE FINISH WHEN YOU ARE HITTING GREENSIDE BUNKER SHOTS. TRY USING A SHORTER SWING FOR GREENSIDE BUNKER SHOT... IT PROVIDES FOR A MORE PREDICTABLE OUTCOME. YOUR BACKSWING LENGTH SHOULD MIRROR THE FOLLOW THROUGH LENGTH.

RACHEL TERESI, LPGA
COG HILL GOLF & COUNTRY CLUB
630.257.5872

Notes

 **DOGLEG**

EACH PLAYER WILL NEED TWO BALLS, A VARIETY OF CHIPPING CLUBS, AND A PUTTER.

THE OBJECTIVE OF "DOGLEG" IS TO CHIP YOUR BALL ONTO THE GREEN, THEN PUTT IT AROUND A DOGLEG AND INTO THE CUP IN AS FEW STROKES AS POSSIBLE.

EACH PLAYER WILL FLIP A COIN TO SEE IF HE WILL BEGIN BY CHIPPING THE "DOGLEG" BALL LEFT (TAILS) OR RIGHT (HEADS) OF THE HOLE. ALL PLAYERS WILL PLAY TO THE SAME HOLE. LET'S SAY, FOR EXAMPLE, YOU FLIP A TAIL. THIS MEANS THAT YOU WILL HAND-TOSS YOUR "DOGLEG BALL" AS CLOSE TO THE LEFT OF THE DESIGNATED HOLE AS POSSIBLE. NEXT, TRY TO CHIP YOUR "PLAY" BALL TO THE LEFT SIDE, AND JUST PAST, THE "DOGLEG BALL" GIVING YOURSELF A STRAIGHT PUTT TO THE HOLE. ALL PLAYERS MUST FIRST FLIP, THEN ALL WILL TOSS THEIR BALL, THEN ALL CHIP, THEN ALL PUTT. REMEMBER THAT YOU MUST COME AROUND THE DESIGNATED LEFT OR RIGHT SIDE OF THE "DOGLEG BALL"... YOU CANNOT "CUT THE CORNER" BY GOING INSIDE OF THE "DOGLEG BALL" WHILE PUTTING TO THE CUP.

PLAY EIGHTEEN HOLES, TOTALING YOUR SCORE(S) AS YOU GO. USING A BLANK SCORECARD MAKES KEEPING TRACK EASY. PAR IS 36! TRY TO BEAT YOUR BEST SCORE OR ENJOY BEATING YOUR FRIENDS.

THE "DOGLEG BALL " TOSS IS VERY IMPORTANT. TRY TO GET IT AS CLOSE TO THE HOLE, ON THE PRESCRIBED SIDE, AS POSSIBLE. IT WILL MAKE YOUR PUTTS MUCH EASIER. "DOGLEG" WILL IMPROVE BOTH YOUR CHIPPING ACCURACY AND YOUR PUTTING FINESSE.

NOEL ALLEN, PGA
THE VILLAGE LINKS
630.469.8180

Notes

CLOSING IN

BEING ABLE TO HAVE
EXCELLENT FEEL FOR YOUR
SHORT PITCH SHOTS
AND TRUSTING YOUR
ABILITY TO PLACE THE BALL
EXACTLY WHERE YOU WANT IT ON THE GREEN IS A SKILL
THAT YOU CAN DEVELOP BY PLAYING "CLOSING IN."

"CLOSING IN" IS A PITCHING GAME THAT IS PLAYED FROM
ABOUT 10-15 YARDS OFF OF THE GREEN. THE OBJECT IS
TO DIRECT YOUR PITCHES, S-L-O-W-L-Y AND DECISIVELY,
CLOSER TO YOUR EVENTUAL TARGET. POINTS ARE
ACCUMULATED AS YOU PITCH.

FIRST, CHOOSE A TARGET PIN ON THE PRACTICE
CHIPPING GREEN. SET 5 BALLS AT A SPOT 10-15 FEET OFF
OF THE GREEN. THEN PLACE A HEAD COVER
FIFTEEN FEET TO THE LEFT OF THE TARGET PIN. ALL
PITCHES MUST LAND BETWEEN THE MARKER AND THE
PIN. YOUR FIRST "SUCCESSFUL" PITCH SHOULD LAND AS
CLOSE TO, BUT NOT LEFT OF, THE MARKER... 1 POINT.
NOW, EACH OF THE REMAINING 4 PITCHES MUST LAND BE-
TWEEN THE PREVIOUSLY PITCHED BALL AND THE PIN...
EACH ONE CLOSING IN ON THE PIN. EACH SUCCESSIVE
PITCH IS WORTH ITSELF (E.G. SECOND PITCH 2 POINTS,
THIRD PITCH, 3 POINTS, ETC.) IF AT ANY POINT A PITCH
LANDS LEFT OF THE PREVIOUSLY PITCHED BALL OR RIGHT
OF THE PIN, THE GAME IS OVER. A PERFECT SCORE IS 15.

PRACTICE "CLOSING IN" FROM THE RIGHT SIDE, ALSO.

DIRECTION CONTROL IS VERY
IMPORTANT IF YOU WISH TO
PLAY COMPETITIVE GOLF.
AROUND THE GREEN,
BE SURE TO HIT THE "SAFE"
SIDE OF THE PIN TO AVOID TROUBLE.

GARY GROH, PGA
BOB O'LINK GOLF CLUB

Notes

 JUMP THE FENCE

 Ingredients

"JUMP THE FENCE" IS A PITCHING AND CHIPPING GAME THAT WILL REFINE YOUR ABILITY TO CONFIDENTLY GET THE BALL IN THE AIR, LAND SOFTLY ON THE GREEN, AND STOP AT THE HOLE... JUST LIKE THE PROS !

THE OBJECTIVE OF "JUMP THE FENCE" IS TO PITCH OR CHIP THE BALL OVER A BARRIER, LAND THE BALL ON THE GREEN, AND HAVE IT STOP SHORT OF THE HOLE, ACCUMULATING POINTS AS YOU JUMP.

PLACE SIX BALLS A FEW FEET OFF OF THE EDGE OF THE GREEN. CHOOSE A TARGET PIN. THEN, PLACE A CLUB BE-TWEEN THE PIN AND THE BALLS, PERPENDICULAR TO THE FLIGHT PATH OF THE BALLS, LOOKING LIKE THIS:

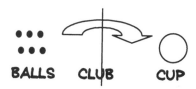

BALLS   CLUB   CUP

PITCHING OR CHIPPING, DEPENDING UPON THE DISTANCE TO THE PIN, HIT EACH OF THE 6 BALLS OVER THE CLUB AND HAVE THEM STOP SHORT OF THE CUP. FOR EACH SUCCESSFUL ATTEMPT, GIVE YOURSELF 2 POINTS. FOR EACH UNSUCCESSFUL ATTEMPT, EITHER SHORT OR LONG, SUBTRACT 1 POINT. A PERFECT SCORE IS A 12. SET A PERSONAL BEST AND TRY TO BEAT IT !!!

 Tips

"JUMP THE FENCE" IS ALSO A GREAT GAME TO PLAY WITH A PARTNER. PLAY TO 21, ALTERNATING SHOTS.

 Chef

DOUG BAUMAN, PGA
BILTMORE COUNTRY CLUB
847.381.6884

Notes

On Perfection

A COLLEGE GOLF COACH ONCE SAID TO ME THAT
"PRACTICE MAKES PERFECT."
I LOOKED AT HIM QUIZZICALLY AND RESPONDED, " I
THINK YOU'RE IN ERROR THERE, COACH ."
HE QUICKLY CORRECTED HIMSELF BY ADDING "YEAH, I
SEE WHERE YOU'RE GOING MIKE, PERFECT PRACTICE
MAKES PERFECT", GRINNING AS IF HE HAD SOLVED
WORLD HUNGER. BUT TO HIS CHAGRIN, I RESPONDED
ONCE AGAIN, "WRONG AGAIN, COACH . DON'T
EXPECT PERFECTION AT ALL. SEEK
EXCELLENCE IN THOUGHT AND ACTION, AND IF
THAT TRANSLATES INTO SUCCESS, WELL THEN,
CONGRADULATIONS."

Notes

ONE ON ONE

"ONE ON ONE" IS A TWO PLAYER TRICK SHOT COMPETITION DESIGNED TO IMPROVE YOUR IMAGINATION, HEIGHTEN CREATIVITY, AND IMPROVE FUNDAMENTALS.

EACH PLAYER WILL NEED ONE BALL AND THEIR ENTIRE SET OF CLUBS. USE A LARGE PRACTICE GREEN WITH MANY HOLES TO CHOOSE FROM.

THE HIGHER HANDICAP PLAYER (PLAYER 1) GOES FIRST. PLAYER 1 CHOOSES A HOLE TO SHOOT TO AND A TYPE OF SHOT THAT HE WILL HIT (PITCH, CHIP, FLOP, TRICK SHOT OVER A BUSH, OFF OF THE PORT-O-LET, ETC.) PLAYER 2 TRIES TO DUPLICATE THE SHOT AND LAND IT WITHIN PLAYER 2. THE WINNER OF THE HOLE CHOOSES THE NEXT SHOT.

HOW TO WIN: EACH HOLE IS WORTH ONE POINT. TWO POINTS IF YOU HOLE OUT. THE FIRST PLAYER TO 18 POINTS WINS.

PRACTICE SHOULD BE FUN AND CHALLENGING !!!

USE YOUR ENTIRE PRE-SHOT ROUTINE AND PICK A SPOT THAT YOU WANT TO LAND... JUST LIKE YOU WOULD OUT ON THE COURSE. REMEMBER, YOU DON'T HAVE TO HIT THE PERFECT SHOT TO WIN. HIT A LOT OF GOOD SHOTS AND YOU WILL FIND YOURSELF INSIDE YOUR OPPONENT MORE OFTEN.

BRYAN LUEDKE, PGA
FOX BEND GOLF COURSE
630.554.3939

Notes

 # THE WET TOWEL

 "THE WET TOWEL" WILL TEACH YOU TO USE A VARIETY OF DIFFERENT CLUBS FOR A VARIETY OF DIFFERENT SITUATIONS.

THE OBJECT OF "THE WET TOWEL" IS TO HIT THREE DIFFERENT SHOTS WITH THE SAME CLUB:

1) A "BELOW THE WAIST" SHOT (ONE THAT NEVER GETS HIGHER THAN YOUR WAIST)
2) A "BELOW THE HEAD" SHOT (ONE THAT IS HIGHER THAN YOUR WAIST, BUT LOWER THAN YOUR HEAD)
3) A "BELOW THE RIM" SHOT (ONE THAT IS HIGHER THAN YOUR HEAD, BUT LOWER THAN TEN FEET)

FROM ANYWHERE AROUND THE GREEN, CHOOSE A CLUB AND HIT EACH OF THE ABOVE SHOTS WITH THAT CLUB. IF YOU ARE ABLE TO HAVE IT LAND ON -NOT STAY ON- THE TOWEL, GIVE YOURSELF 1 POINT. TRY TO SEE HOW MANY POINTS YOU CAN ACCUMULATE WITH TWENTY SHOTS.

TRY MANY DIFFERENT SHOTS! GET RISKY!

 BEING VERSATILE WITH MANY DIFFERENT CLUBS IS VERY IMPORTANT. BECOMING PROFICIENT AT "THE WET TOWEL" WILL BOOST YOUR CONFIDENCE, TEACH YOU TO BE VERY CREATIVE AROUND THE GREEN, AND WILL KEEP YOUR OPPONENT ON HIS TOES AS HE ADMIRES YOUR VERSATILITY.

 TI M O'NEAL, PGA
NORTH SHORE COUNTRY CLUB
847.724.9240

Notes

 **Recipe** **ZERO**

 **Ingredients**

"ZERO" IS A CHIPPING AND PUTTING GAME THAT WILL IMPROVE YOUR FEEL AND ACCURACY AROUND THE GREEN AND BOOST YOUR CONFIDENCE TO "ONE PUTT FOR THE WIN."

THE OBJECTIVE OF "ZERO" IS TO GET UP AND DOWN CONSISTENTLY AND, BY DOING SO, WIN THE GAME. "ZERO" IS BEST PLAYED WITH 3-4 PLAYERS.

EACH PLAYER PLACES 3 BALLS THREE FEET OFF OF THE EDGE OF THE GREEN. EACH PLAYER PLAYS INDEPENDENTLY FROM EACH OTHER, BY ATTEMPTING TO CHIP UP AND PUTT DOWN IN TWO TOTAL STROKES. IF THE PLAYER SUCCESSFULLY GETS ALL THREE BALLS UP AND DOWN, HE MAY REMOVE ONE BALL AND CONTINUE WITH THE REMAINING 2 BALLS. ONCE AGAIN, IF HE IS SUCCESSFUL GETTING UP AND DOWN WITH 2 BALLS, HE MAY REMOVE ONE AND ATTEMPT THE LAST BALL. IF, AT ANY POINT, A PLAYER CANNOT GET UP & DOWN WITH ALL OF THE BALLS HE HAS LEFT, HE MUST ADD A BALL AND CONTINUE. THE FIRST PLAYER TO ZERO BALLS WINS THE GAME.

 **Tips**

WHILE "ZERO" IS SELF-PACED, AND TENDS TO GET "QUICK", THE MORE THAT YOU CAN KEEP A STEADY, CONSISTENT PACE THE BETTER OFF YOU WILL BE. KEEP YOUR EMOTIONS IN CHECK!

 **Chef**

CAROL RHOADES, LPGA
GOLF GALAXY
847.882.3828

Notes

BUNKER HILL

"BUNKER HILL" IS A GREAT GAME TO REFINE YOUR BUNKER SHOTS AND PRACTICE GETTING OUT TO DIFFERENT DISTANCES.

ON THE GREEN, LAY THREE CLUBS PERPENDICULAR TO THE PRACTICE BUNKER. THE FIRST IS 8 YARDS FROM THE BUNKER, THE SECOND IS 12 YARDS FROM THE BUNKER, AND THE THIRD, 18 YARDS. EACH CLUB REPRESENTS A DISTANCE TO CARRY THE BALL.

FIRST, HIT FIVE BALLS TO THE 8 YARD CLUB (IF YOU ARE ACCURATE, THE CLUB SHOULD STOP THE BALL). THEN HIT FIVE BALLS TO THE 12 YARD MARKER , AND FINALLY 5 TO THE 18 YARD MARKER. GIVE YOURSELF ONE POINT FOR EACH TARGET HIT. A PERFECT SCORE IS 15, BUT ANYTHING ABOVE 11 IS DARN GOOD. KEEP TRACK OF YOUR BEST SCORE AND TRY TO BEAT IT.

"BUNKER HILL" IS ALSO GREAT FUN, AND CHALLENGING, AS A COMPETITION WITH ANOTHER PLAYER.

THE KEY TO A SUCCESSFUL BUNKER SHOT IS THE OPENING OF THE CLUBFACE. BE SURE, ALSO, TO SWING THROUGH THE IMPACT POINT... DON'T STOP YOUR SWING AT THE BALL . DON'T BE AFRAID OF SAND !!!

JOHN PARSONS, PGA
SCHAUMBURG GOLF CLUB
847.885.9000

Notes

MULTIPLICITY

"MULTIPLICITY" WILL HELP YOU TO HIT A VARIETY OF GREENSIDE CHIPS, PITCHES, AND BUNKER SHOTS WITH A GREATER SENSE OF CONFIDENCE AND TRUST.

IF YOU PLAY "MULTIPLICITY" ALONE, FIRST MAKE A SIX FOOT CIRCLE AROUND THE PIN WITH SOME SPARE TEES. THIS CIRCLE IS YOUR TARGET AREA. IF YOU ARE PLAYING WITH A PARTNER, YOU DON'T NEED A CIRCLE, AS IT IS PLAYED "CLOSER TO THE PIN." EACH PLAYER NEEDS TO CARRY A SW, PW, 9I, 8I, AND 7I, WITH THEM AS THEY WORK THEIR WAY AROUND THE GREEN.

THE OBJECT OF THE GAME IS TO HIT THE BALL AS CLOSE TO THE PIN (AND, HOPEFULLY IN) AS POSSIBLE WHILE ACCUMULATING POINTS. ONE GAME IS 9 SHOTS. THE PLAYER WITH THE MOST POINTS AT THE END, WINS.

PLAYER ONE CALLS A SHOT, ANY SHOT, AND ATTEMPTS TO HIT THE SHOT AT THE PIN. PLAYER TWO THEN FOLLOWS SUIT. WHOEVER IS CLOSER TO THE PIN, SCORES ONE POINT. THE LOSER OF THAT SHOT PICKS THE NEXT SHOT, ANY SHOT. IF PLAYING ALONE, HIT ALL 9 SHOTS, FROM A MULTIPLICITY OF SPOTS, THEN TOTAL THE NUMBER OF SHOTS THAT LAND IN THE SIX-FOOT TARGET CIRCLE. TRY TO BEAT YOUR PERSONAL BEST!

WHEN PRACTICING, IT IS VERY IMPORTANT TO HIT THE SHOTS THAT YOU WILL FACE ON THE COURSE. IT IS THIS TYPE OF "REALITY PRACTICE" THAT WILL HELP YOU TO HIT THOSE DIFFICULT SHOTS WHEN IT REALLY COUNTS.

TIM SURLAS, PGA
CHICAGO GOLF CLUB

Notes

 **CRUMBLE**

 "CRUMBLE" IS A TWO PLAYER GREENSIDE GAME THAT CAN BE PLAYED USING VIRTUALLY ANY CLUB IN ANY SITUATION.

THE OBJECT OF "CRUMBLE" IS TO OUT-CHIP, PUTT, OR PITCH YOUR OPPONENT AND FORCE HIM TO "CRUMBLE" UNDER THE PRESSURE.

EACH PLAYER PLAYS WITH TWO BALLS. PLAYER ONE SHOOTS FIRST TO A DESIGNATED HOLE. THEN, PLAYER TWO SHOOTS BOTH OF HIS BALLS TO THE HOLE. FOLLOWED BY PLAYER ONE'S SECOND BALL (THE REASON FOR THE ORDER IS THERE IS A SLIGHT DISADVANTAGE TO GOING FIRST AND SHOWING THE LINE. THIS DISADVANTAGE IS OFFSET BY GOING LAST).

SCORING

1 POINT...	CLOSEST BALL
2 POINTS...	2 CLOSEST BALLS (BY ONE PLAYER)
EXTRA POINT...	HOLED SHOT

SO, THE MAXIMUM NUMBER OF POINTS FOR A PLAYER PER ROUND IS 4. FIRST PLAYER TO GAIN A 7 POINT ADVANTAGE WINS.

 COMPETITIVE PRACTICE GAMES BUILD COMPETITIVE COMPOSURE AND EXPERIENCE IN A CONTROLLED SETTING. BECOMING "COOL" IN PRACTICE SHOULD HELP THE PLAYER TO AVOID "CRUMBLING" DURING COMPETITION.

 MICHAEL SMALL, PGA
THE UNIVERSITY OF ILLINOIS
217.333.8604

Notes

On Play

THERE ARE TWO DISTINCT WAYS OF THINKING
WITH A GOLF CLUB IN YOUR HAND.
ONE IS FUN, AND AWARE,
AND ARTISTIC, AND FEELY,
AND ACCEPTING, AND PLAYFUL.
THE OTHER IS SCIENTIFIC, AND ANGULAR,
AND JUDGMENTAL, AND GRITTY,
AND EXACT, AND PROFESSORIAL.
IF YOU WANT TO PLAY
YOUR BEST OUT ON THE COURSE,
DO YOUR BEST TO THINK THE FIRST WAY.

Notes

BETCHA CAN'T

"BETCHA" CAN'T IS A TWO PLAYER GAME THAT WILL TEST YOUR SHOT-MAKING ABILITY AND ANSWER THE QUESTION, "DO YA' FEEL LUCKY, WELL, DO YA?"

PLAYER ONE STARTS OUT BY CALLING A REASONABLY RIDICULOUS SHOT, LIKE "I CAN HIT THIS BALL (WHICH LIES IN DEEP ROUGH ABOUT FIFTEEN YARDS OFF OF THE EDGE OF THE GREEN) WITH A FOUR IRON ONTO THE GREEN AND PUTT OUT IN THREE SHOTS." IF PLAYER TWO THINKS HE CAN HIT THE "CALLED" SHOT IN FEWER STROKES, HE CAN CALL, "I CAN MAKE THAT CALL IN TWO STROKES." AT ANY POINT, EITHER PLAYER CAN CALL "BETCHA CAN'T" WHICH AUTOMATICALLY FORCES THE PLAYER TO HIT THE CALLED SHOT IN THE CALLED AMOUNT OF STROKES. ONCE A PLAYER IS "CALLED," HE MUST EXECUTE THE CALL.

A SUCCESSFUL EXECUTION IN THE CALLED NUMBER OF STROKES IS WORTH 3 POINTS. FAILURE TO EXECUTE THE SHOT RESULTS IN A LOSS OF 1 POINT.

THE FIRST PLAYER TO 18 POINTS WINS.

"BETCHA CAN'T" TAKES GUTS. DON'T BE AFRAID TO TRY SHOTS THAT SEEM TOO DIFFICULT... IT IS ONLY BY STRETCHING YOUR LIMITS THAT YOU IMPROVE.

BILLY NESTEL, PGA
CANTIGNY GOLF CLUB
630.260.8276

Notes

FIELD GOAL

"FIELD GOAL" IS DESIGNED TO HELP PLAYERS TO IMPROVE THEIR LOFT AND DIRECTION CONTROL WITH SHORT PITCH AND CHIP SHOTS.

THE OBJECTIVE OF "FIELD GOAL" IS FOR THE PLAYER TO CHIP OR PITCH A PREDETERMINED SHOT AT A PREDETERMINED TARGET FOR POINTS.

PLACE NINE BALLS IN AN OPEN PRACTICE AREA. THEN, TAKE TWO HEAD COVERS OFF OF YOUR WOODS AND PLACE THEM ON THE GROUND ABOUT TWENTY FEET AWAY, TEN FEET APART. THE HEAD COVERS BECOME YOUR "GOALPOSTS." YOU MAY ONLY USE THREE CLUBS: A HIGH LOFT WEDGE, A 9 IRON AND A 7 IRON. HIT THREE BALLS WITH EACH CLUB, THE HIGH, MEDIUM, AND LOW TRAJECTORY SHOT, BETWEEN THE GOAL POST FOR A "FIELD GOAL." EACH SUCCESSFUL SHOT IS WORTH 3 POINTS FOR A TOTAL POSSIBLE 27 POINTS.

SEE HOW CLOSE TO 27 YOU CAN COME !!!

TO INCREASE THE DIFFICULTY OF "FIELD GOAL," MOVE THE GOALPOSTS CLOSER TOGETHER. ALSO, DO NOT HIT ALL THREE WEDGES, 9 IRONS, AND 7 IRONS IN A ROW. ROTATE CLUBS AS YOU WOULD OUT ON THE GOLF COURSE.

JOHN CLELAND, PGA
BUTTERFIELD COUNTRY CLUB
630.323.1307

Notes

 **OVER EASY**

 "OVER EASY" IS A GREAT BUNKER AND PUTTING GAME THAT REQUIRES YOU TO HIT SAND SHOTS THAT YOU TYPICALLY FACE ON THE COURSE & PUTT OUT !

TAKE THREE BALLS AND YOUR SAND WEDGE AND MOSEY INTO A GREENSIDE PRACTICE BUNKER. TAKE ONE OF THE BALLS AND GIVE YOURSELF AN EASY, FLUFFY, SOFT LIE. THEN TAKE THE SECOND BALL AND GIVE YOURSELF A MODERATELY DIFFICULT LIE... MAYBE, IN A FOOTMARK OR SLIGHTLY DOWNHILL. LASTLY, WITH YOUR LAST BALL GIVE YOURSELF A VERY DIFFICULT LIE... UNDER A LIP, A FRIED EGG, OR A SEVERE SLOPE.

IN ORDER TO GAIN POINTS, YOU MUST GET UP & DOWN FROM THE RESPECTIVE LIES. IF NOT, YOU "WASTED" A GREAT SAND SHOT. THE EASY LIE IS WORTH ONE POINT, THE MODERATE IS WORTH TWO, AND THE DIFFICULT LIE IS WORTH THREE POINTS. A PERFECT SCORE IS A SIX. PLAY SIX ROUNDS AND TOTAL YOUR SCORE. IF YOU CAN SCORE IN THE 30'S YOU ARE DOING VERY WELL ! IN THE 20'S, GOOD. IN THE TEENS, KEEP WORKING.

 IMAGINE TRYING TO "SWIPE" A DOLLAR BILL OUT FROM UNDER YOUR BALL WHEN HITTING OUT OF THE BUNKER. THIS MOTION IS PERFECT FOR A GREAT SAND SHOT. HIT DOWN 1-2" BEHIND THE BALL.

 CHRIS HEASLEY, PGA
NIKE GOLF LEARNING CENTER
708.449.6767

Notes

 **Recipe**

WORST BALL SCRAMBLE

 **Ingredients**

"WORST BALL SCRAMBLE" IS EITHER A ONE, TWO, OR THREE PLAYER GAME THAT FORCES THE PLAYER TO "STAY IN THE GAME" AND FOCUS, ESPECIALLY FOLLOWING A POOR SHORT GAME SHOT.

THE OBJECTIVE IS TO PLAY 18 HOLES, USING TWO BALLS, ALWAYS COUNTING THE WORST OF THE TWO, WHILE TRYING TO CARD THE LOWEST SCORE POSSIBLE.

"WBS" IS PLAYED ON AND AROUND THE PRACTICE GREEN. PLAYER ONE CALLS A SHOT THAT HE, AND ALL COMPETITORS MUST ALL PLAY. FOR EXAMPLE, LET'S USE A 20 YARD PITCH SHOT: PLAYER "A" PITCHES ONE TO 5 FEET AND ONE BARELY ON THE FRINGE, HE MUST PLAY THE SHOT ON THE FRINGE; HE THEN CHIPS ONE TO 3 FEET AND BLOWS A PUTT PAST 6 FEET; HE MUST PLAY THE SIX FOOT PUTT, ETC. THE SAME RULES APPLY TO ALL PLAYERS.

AFTER EACH PLAYER HAS HOLED OUT, RECORD ALL SCORES. THE PLAYER WITH THE LOWEST SCORE FOR THAT HOLE HAS HONORS AND CALLS THE NEXT SHOT.

 **Tips**

"WBS" FORCES PLAYERS TO STAY FOCUSED FOR BOTH SHOTS. AS ON THE GOLF COURSE, A PLAYER SHOULDN'T "GIVE UP" FOLLOWING A POOR HIT.

 **Chef**

JIM VOGT, PGA
THE HIGHLANDS OF ELGIN
847.931.6102

Notes

 **MATCH THIS**

 "MATCH THIS" IS A TWO PLAYER, MATCH PLAY, SHORT- GAME GAME THAT IMPROVES ALL OF THE PLAYER'S GREENSIDE SHOT-MAKING AND PUTTING SKILLS.

THE OBJECT OF "MATCH THIS" IS TO OUTSCORE YOUR OPPONENT, ONE HOLE AT A TIME. THIS IS AN EIGHTEEN HOLE GAME ON AND AROUND THE PRACTICE GREEN.

THE HIGHER HANDICAP PLAYER CALLS A GREENSIDE OR BUNKER SHOT TO START THE MATCH. BOTH PLAYERS THEN, INDEPENDENTLY, PLAY OUT THAT SHOT. THE PLAYER WITH THE LOWER TOTAL NUMBER OF STROKES FOR THE HOLE GETS ONE POINT. THE LOSER OF THE H OLE RECEIVES "HONORS" FOR THE NEXT HOLE BY CALLING THE NEXT SHOT. REPEAT UNTIL YOU HAVE PLAYED EIGHTEEN HOLES (REFER TO USGA MATCH PLAY RULES FOR SPECIFICS).

THE PLAYER THAT WINS THE MAJORITY OF THE EIGHTEEN HOLES IS DECLARED THE WINNER OF THE MATCH. TIES ARE DECIDED BY A PLAYOFF.

 TO INCREASE THE DRAMA OF "MATCH THIS," THE "HONORS" PLAYER MAY BE ALLOWED TO CALL BOTH THE SHOT AND THE CLUB. GIMMES ARE ALLOWED.

 SCOTT SANDFORT, PGA
ELGIN COUNTRY CLUB
847.741.2707

Notes

 # CENTURY

 **"CENTURY"** IS A ONE OR MULTI-PERSON GAME THAT WILL DEVELOP YOUR ABILITY TO GET UP & DOWN FROM A VARIETY OF PLACES AROUND THE GREEN AND FROM THE GREENSIDE BUNKERS.

THE OBJECTIVE OF "CENTURY" IS TO GET ONTO THE GREEN AND PUTT OUT IN AS FEW STROKES AS POSSIBLE.

EACH PLAYER PLAYS THREE BALLS AND USES THE CLUB OF HIS CHOICE. THE FIRST SPOT FROM WHICH THE PLAYERS HIT AND THE TARGET PIN IS CHOSEN BY THE BEST-LOOKING PLAYER. THE SUBSEQUENT ORDER IS BY ROTATION. ALL PLAYERS WILL FIRST CHIP OR PITCH ONTO THE GREEN. IF A PLAYER FAILS TO LAND THE GREEN WITH HIS FIRST SHOT OF EACH SET, THAT BALL - NOT THE PLAYER - IS AUTOMATICALLY DISQUALIFIED FOR THAT SET. ONCE ON THE GREEN, EACH PLAYER MUST PUTT OUT WITH EACH QUALIFIED BALL. SCORING OF ALL HOLED BALLS IS AS FOLLOWS:

> 10 POINTS... HOLED CHIP OR PITCH
> 5 POINTS... UP & DOWN (ONE PUTT)
> 2 POINTS.... UP & 2 PUTTS
> -3 POINTS... UP & MORE THAN 2 PUTTS

THE FIRST PLAYER TO ACCUMULATE 100 POINTS WINS. SCORES SHOULD BE TALLIED AND SHARED BEFORE EACH SET. IF PLAYING ALONE, YOUR GOAL SHOULD BE TO FINISH IN 10 SETS OR LESS.

 CONCENTRATING ON THE FIRST SHOT IS VERY IMPORTANT. NOT ONLY TO GET CLOSE, BUT TO AVOID THE BALL FROM BEING DISQUALIFIED. BE SMART.

 **JASON ASLANIAN, PGA**
BARRINGTON HILLS COUNTRY CLUB
847.381.4212

Notes

HOLE IN ONE

"HOLE IN ONE" IS AN EXCELLENT PRACTICE GAME THAT GIVES THE PLAYER THE CHANCE TO HIT FROM THREE DIFFERENT GREENSIDE SPOTS THAT SIMULATE REAL COURSE-LIKE SITUATIONS.

FIRST, USING GOLF TEES, CREATE A SIX-FOOT DIAMETER CIRCLE AROUND ONE OF THE HOLES ON THE PRACTICE GREEN. THIS IS YOUR TARGET.

YOUR HITTING SPOTS ARE: BUNKER, THREE FEET OFF OF THE GREEN, AND A 20 YARD PITCH SHOT. TAKE FOUR BALLS TO THE BUNKER AND PITCH ALL FOUR ONTO THE GREEN, TRYING TO HAVE THEM STOP WITHIN THE TARGET CIRCLE. PITCH FROM TWENTY YARDS WITH THE SAME TARGET. AND LASTLY, CHIP FROM OFF OF THE GREEN. KEEP TRACK OF YOUR RESULTS.

SCORING CHART

BIRDIE (-1) ...	3 OUT OF 4 IN CIRCLE
PAR (0)...	2 OUT OF 4 IN CIRCLE
BOGEY (+1)...	1 OUT OF 4 IN CIRCLE
DOUBLE BOGEY (+2)...	0 OUT OF 4 IN CIRCLE

REPEAT THIS CYCLE SIX TIMES TO COMPLETE EIGHTEEN HOLES. SHOOT FOR UNDER PAR, BUT ACCEPT YOUR BEST.

BE SURE NOT TO GET CAUGHT IN THE "RAPID FIRE TRAP" WITH THESE SHOTS. AFTER EACH SHOT, STEP BACK AND COMPLETE YOUR FULL ROUTINE BEFORE YOU SWING. PRACTICE LIKE YOU ARE GOING TO PLAY ON THE COURSE, OF COURSE.

MATT ABRAMAVICIUS, PGA
MARENGO RIDGE GOLF CLUB
815.923.2332

Notes

Notes

Notes

Notes

Notes

Notes

Notes

Notes

Notes

Notes

Notes

Notes